THE PLAY'S THE THING 2

David Muncaster

Playscript reviews published in
Amateur Stage Magazine 2012 - 2013

I0133174

SILVERMOON PUBLISHING
London
www.silvermoonpublishing.co.uk

THE PLAY'S THE THING

First published in Great Britain in December 2013
by Silvermoon Publishing
3rd Floor, 207 Regent Street, London, W1B 3HH

Typeset by Douglas Mayo

A CIP catalogue record for this book is available from the British
Library.

ISBN 978 1 840 94944 5

DAVID MUNCASTER

Theatre has been part of David's life ever since his school days. He is on record for saying that drama studies were just about the only thing he was any good at, but turned down an opportunity to work at the Nottingham Playhouse as an Assistant Stage Manager because the cost of rent, food and bus fare were greater than the salary on offer. Instead he immersed himself into amateur theatre where he has done everything with the exception of prompt; which he wouldn't do "for all the tea in China"!

He began writing as a teenager, firstly lyrics for a rock band then articles for a student magazine before starting work on his first book. It took a surprising long time before David finally combined his passion for theatre with writing but his first play, *Call Girls* was an immediate success being published by New Theatre Publications and having performances in both the UK and the USA. Since then there have been hundreds of performances of David's work around the world by both amateur and professional companies with his festival friendly one act plays regularly winning awards.

In 2010 he answered an advertisement in *Amateur Stage* for a playscript reviewer and with an average of eight plays a month his reviews have become one of the most popular features in the magazine.

David lives in Cheshire where he is an active participant for two amateur groups and an enthusiastic supporter of all forms of theatre.

www.davidmuncaster.com

For Margaret

Contents

CONTENTS

CONTENTS

INTRODUCTION

Picking the right play for your amateur theatre company is key to your success not only in terms of audience reaction, but also to ensure your membership continues to thrive. This reference guide should be the first port of call for any group as David's concise reviews are written with a thorough comprehension of the needs of amateur groups ensuring you get a clear understanding of the entire play in just a few short paragraphs.

The Playscript Review section of Amateur Stage magazine is always one of the most popular monthly features which helps groups find titles they may never have considered in the past.

As editor of Amateur Stage magazine it is always a pleasure to read David's reviews and I am sure this second volume will be of great use to groups nationwide in their quest to present exciting, thought-provoking and challenging theatre.

Julian Cound
Editor
Amateur Stage magazine

Reviews
2012 - 2013

55 DAYS

Author: Howard Brenton
Publisher: Nick Hern Books
ISBN NO: 9781842422287
Cast: 13M 2F with doubling
Type: Full Length

In 1648 London witnessed a military coup. After parliament voted against trying King Charles I on charges of treason, an army gathered in Hyde Park and prepared to make their move on Westminster. However, one man was missing. The question on everyone's lips at the start of Howard Breton's play is "Where is Oliver Cromwell?" The answer is Pontefract, though his reasons for being there are unclear. The threat from the Scots, still loyal to the king, is negligible but Cromwell seems hesitant about making the journey south, claiming that he is waiting for God's word. Eventually he asks Lord Fairfax to order him to go. Lord Fairfax obliges.

Meanwhile, on the Isle of Wight, Charles I is playing bowls. In a display of arrogance that we will see a lot more of before the end of the play, the King freely admits that his promise to parliament that he would abolish bishops was a lie intended to get the Presbyterians to vote for him. If he were to be restored to his position of head of the church, the bishops would remain and it is the Presbyterians that would be thrown into prison.

The extremists call for Charles I to be beheaded but Cromwell wants a compromise: a country that retains the monarchy but where to power lies with parliament. Charles I will have none of this and, when he is eventually brought to court to face charges of treason, his response is to demand on what authority is he being tried. What lawful authority? Even Cromwell questions whether a king can be tried for treason against himself but, in a secret meeting between the two, Charles I's arrogance is his undoing.

With such a large number of characters, 55 Days is surely it beyond the means of most amateur groups and the story is so complex it can be quite hard work but, at its heart, is a compelling courtroom drama that gives us a glimpse into a remarkable period in Britain's history.

AGATHA CRUSTY AND THE VILLAGE HALL MURDERS

Author: Derek Webb
Publisher: New Theatre Publications
ISBN NO: 9781840948929
Cast: 4M 6F or 3M 7F
Type: Full Length

Agatha Crusty is a celebrated crime novelist who has been invited by her sister in law, Alice, to spend a few days with her in the village of Chortelby. On her arrival she finds that there have recently been a number of unexplained deaths and soon becomes caught up in a murder investigation being conducted by the incompetent Inspector Twigg.

The script is brimming with lots of wonderful word play. I particularly enjoyed Inspector Twigg's explanation of the components of a murder enquiry: there must be Motive, Opportunity and Method, which will require: Detection, Application and Dedication in order to produce: Killers In Dock Sooner. The characters' names also provide Inspector Twigg with plenty of opportunity to get himself in a muddle with lines like, "Isn't it true that you refused to let Carrie marry Barry, Harry?"

Agatha is, of course, the archetypal meddling crime writer but Twigg is so incompetent he is glad of her help. As the members of the village hall committee are bumped off one by one, motives and theories abound; but Agatha calmly examines the evidence until we reach the inevitable the-murderer-is-someone-in-this-room scene.

This is a play that is going to delight anyone who revels in a traditional comedy/murder with lots of witty lines and funny scenes. But there is also a genuine murder plot and I am sure that audiences will enjoy separating the red herrings from the real clues.

Finally, I have to say that I have read enough of Derek Webb's comedies to know that he never disappoints but he had me going with this one. With an Inspector Twigg there is an obvious joke that has to be in there somewhere but he makes us wait until the very last page. It does, however, add to the sense of satisfaction when the curtain falls; the play just wouldn't have been complete without a Special Branch reference!

ALI BABA
Author: Stephen Curtis
Publisher: Spotlight Publications
ISBN NO: 9781907303393
Cast: 8M 9F
Type: Pantomime

Rhum Baba is an unhappy woman. Ali has been out all night even though it is their wedding anniversary and she doesn't have two shekels to rub together: not enough to buy but a few fish heads. However, when Ali appears with jewels and gold bars that, er, fell off the back of a camel it seems that their troubles are over.

Rhum Baba heads to the market to treat herself to a slave and gets herself a bargain in the diligent but unable to speak, Jellipanta. But it seems that her new slave cannot bear to be parted from her best friend, Morgiana, and the soft centred Rhum Baba agrees to buy them both. Ali is mortified. He knows that the loot is stolen and when the robbers get to hear that he has come into money they are bound to put two and two together.

Abdul Al Haqq is indeed angry. So angry, in fact, that some directors may feel his dialogue is unsuitable for a family audience. This, together with Rhum Baba's talk of having a "boob job" are two examples of where this script, which appears to have been written to appeal to very young people, contains elements more suited to a pantomime targeted at an older audience.

That said, there are some good moments. I particularly enjoyed some of the song lyrics, but I fear that this is not enough to make this version of Ali Baba stand out from the competition.

ALL BALLS AND ASHES
Author: Mark Robberts
Publisher: Playstage
ISBN NO: 9781907147272
Cast: 6M 5F
Type: Full Length

A few months ago a local theatre did some promotion saying that anyone who liked Last of the Summer Wine would enjoy their current production. Up until then I had been undecided about going to see it but that was enough for me to make up my mind: I steered clear. I mention this because it is impossible to completely ignore personal penchants when reviewing scripts and All Balls and Ashes has clearly been written with lovers of the long running TV series in mind, to the extent that the three main characters could very easily be Foggy, Compo and Clegg. Indeed, the notes in the script tell us that the play was originally written as an intended pilot to replace LOTSW until the BBC relented and commissioned another series.

We are in the village of Greenbridge on the border of Yorkshire and Lancashire. The Great Umpire in the Sky has called "over" on Seth 'Hot Balls' Hegginbotham: he has bowled his last. Unfortunately, this was whilst practising his bowling in the bedroom and, forgetting to let go of the ball, he finished his run up at the bottom of the stairs. Now his best friends; Frank, George and Eli, are planning to carry out his last wish: to have his ashes scattered on the village cricket green.

The problem is that Seth's widow, Freda, will have none of it. She has the ashes in an urn that she takes to bed with her every night and has no intention of allowing them to be scattered anywhere. If the trio are going to carry out their friend's wish they are going to have to find a way to purloin Seth's ashes without Freda finding out.

Eli is the unfortunate purloiner and, though he successfully swaps the ashes for the scrapings from the dog grate, he drops his tin hat and scares Freda out of her wits in the process. Nevertheless, the three of them proceed to the cricket field and scatter the ashes in a bizarre ceremony before retiring to the pub to celebrate their success. It is here that they learn that, due to recent boundary changes, they have scattered their friend in Lancashire!

With the help of the vicar and a carpet sweeper they are able to rectify their error but by this time Freda has decided that the vision in a tin hat was a sign that she should let Seth have his way and she scatters the substitute ashes. Then, as the trio look on, a steady flow of women come to pay their respects to Seth making them realise that his nickname had nothing to do with his bowling ability.

There are elements in this script that I enjoyed. Dolly and Vera, who always finish.....

......each other's sentences, made me smile and there is also plenty of

18

physical comedy. I can imagine a lot of fun as the vicar's carpet sweeper is accompanied by our trio doing the shake 'n' vac dance. I suppose to sum up I have to say that if you like Last of the Summer Wine you will like All Balls and Ashes.

ARMS FLOATING LIKE SEAWEED
Author: Scott Marshall
Publisher: Kenyon Deane
ISBN NO: 9780715504208
Cast: 3F
Type: One Act

Arms Floating Like Seaweed is a tender play that has a prodigal daughter returning to her home for her father's funeral. Shannon lives in America and, though she doesn't sound like much of a high flier, she puts her stay-at-home sister in the shade. Connie is a little younger and a little more innocent. She is also more respectful to their mother, Mam, who does not appreciate the attitude that Shannon has adopted since she returned.

Scott Marshall does well to bring the characters to life right from the very start and their affection for each other – or is it just for their memories - is immediately apparent. Soon we become aware that Shannon is hiding something; something to do with her husband, Jerry. Mam and Connie both try to get it out of her but she holds back.

Instead she tells a story about a woman whom she met at a party who revealed all her innermost thoughts and fears. Shannon believes that the woman did the right thing. If you have a secret to unfold tell it to a stranger, not a friend. But having told the story she suddenly unburdens herself. The reason that Jerry hasn't come to the funeral is that he is seriously ill. On top of this, Shannon is three months pregnant and she has something she wants to ask Connie. We then find that Mam also has secrets: ones that she has kept for 42 years, and Connie finds herself on the brink of making a momentous decision.

Scott Marshall has an exceptional ability to draw us into his characters so that we think of them as though they were old friends. Dramatic story lines and plot twists can make for exciting plays but a simple tale about people who get under our skin can be so affecting. This is another excellent festival ready play from this talented author.

BEFORE THE PARTY
Author: Rodney Ackland based on a short story by W Somerset Maugham
Publisher: Oberon Modern Plays
ISBN NO: 9781849434423
Cast: 2M 5F
Type: Full Length

This play has been published following its revival in 2013, sixty-four years after it was first performed in the West End. Rodney Ackland was a very popular playwright at the time having several plays on in the West End including his first play, Improper People, which he started writing at the age of fifteen.

Laura is recently widowed and has returned from Africa to be with her family who are trying to get back to normal following the end of the war. Here she has met David whom, unbeknownst to her family, she plans to marry. However, as the play begins, she appears to have changed her mind and David is demanding to know what prompted this decision.

In order to speak to Laura, David has had to force himself into her bedroom where Laura's elder sister, Kathleen, is appalled to find them. "You're not in Africa now." she tells her sister. Kathleen's pompous outrage seems to bring Laura and David together and the marriage is back on; but first they have to endure a party, that her mother has arranged, with the local bishop being one of the guests. Laura promises David that she will announce their plan to get married "after the party" but events take an unexpected turn and the news comes out earlier than planned.

The mother, Blanche, is an interesting character. For example she says that she hates cruelty to animals, therefore she does not want her enjoyment of foie gras spoilt by knowing how it is made. It doesn't seem to occur to her to stop eating it. Aubrey, the father, is another odd one. A lawyer, he tells David that he will only handle "clean" divorces: ones involving cruelty, drunkenness or lunacy. He would only handle a sexual divorce if the misconduct had been performed "purely as a formality".

It will come as no surprise that the whole family, with the exception of Laura and her young sister, Susan, are the most terrible snobs. It is the kind of snobbishness especially prevalent in people who secretly believe they are not quite up to the standard of those that they admire the most and they are dead set against Laura marrying David, a common travelling salesman.

We then learn the reason for Laura's earlier change of heart. The official story is that her first husband died of malaria but there are rumours that he committed suicide. The truth is far worse: Laura killed him when she returned from a trip and found the supposedly reformed alcoholic unconscious from drink. Then, in one final twist, the family have found in Who's Who that David is heir to a fortune and are now wholly in favour of the marriage!

I can understand why this almost forgotten play was chosen to be revived. After all, plays such as Patrick Hamilton's Gaslight never cease to be popular, and I have no doubt that audiences will enjoy the preposterous melodrama in Before The Party.

BETTER THAN THE REAL THING
Author: John Ward
Publisher: Unpublished
ISBN NO: None
Cast: 5M 5F plus others
Type: Full Length

One piece of advice often given out to any aspiring playwright is, before even putting finger to keyboard, to see lots of plays. It is natural, then, that the types of play the writer sees will influence the types of plays he writes. My guess is that John Ward has seen a lot of Whitehall type farces.

Enthusiasts for this genre will be pleased, when the curtain rises, to find themselves in the comfortable setting of a village rectory. Here, members of rival flower arranging societies are competing to have a display in the parish church. Add to this mix the rector's wife enjoying a dangerous liaison with the gardener and a large bottle of spring water that is in reality, gin, and everything is nicely set up in the first dozen or so pages.

With the competing societies unwilling to work together, one even going so far as to accuse the other of using artificial flowers, the rector decides to refer the matter to a higher authority: the archdeacon no less. Except that the archdeacon is currently in Japan making it possible for the rector to get his friend, Robert to impersonate him.

Robert declares that neither society will do the display and produces a female priest that he claims to have met in Japan. This is Fiona who has painted her face white and is wearing a kimono and black wig. How anyone would imagine that this is how a Japanese Christian priest would dress is beyond me but it seems to convince the ladies from the flower arranging societies.

Here the author attempts to derive humour from Fiona making infantile noises that she imagines sound like the Japanese language and, for me, the play reaches a low point from which it never really recovers. I'm sure that the author would argue that the joke is on Fiona and that he isn't making fun of Japanese language and culture but it is a joke that has worn thin. For the record, the second act sees the real archdeacon turn up, the rector's gin smuggling racket exposed and the flower arranging societies finally agreeing to work together.

The play is not entirely without merit. The pace keeps the action moving along swiftly and there are large numbers of theatre goers who enjoy a traditional farce. However, if this writer wants to see his work more widely appreciated, I'd recommend that he take a more modern outlook.

BISCUITS
Author: Graham J Evans
Publisher: Drama Association of Wales
ISBN NO: 9781908575048
Cast: 5M 2F
Ttpe: One Act

It is 1361 and King Edward the Third has decreed that "Good and lawful men be appointed in every county to guard the peace". Henry of Grosmont is one of those men and he has instructed William, his Clerk of Works, to build a new courthouse. This causes William a problem: right where the front door should be lives Mad Nerys who is a witch and not to be trifled with.

Gerald, lecherous monk and legal adviser to Henry of Groswold, agrees to help William, no doubt influenced by William's buxom daughter, Gwen.

Meanwhile, Nigel, by virtue of being handed a magical sword by a Lady of the Lake, claims to be the re-incarnation of Llewelyn Ap Gruffold, ruler of all Wales. However, it is a disputed claim because there were no witnesses to this event and he is unable to produce the sword in question. Nevertheless he plans to storm Henry of Grosmont's castle and reclaim it for the Welsh. Eventually! For now, thinking it better to start small, he will have to make do with storming the courthouse. The trouble is, the courthouse hasn't been built and Nigel ends up storming Mad Nerys' hovel.

Now homeless, Mad Nerys is brought to William's house along with Beelzebub, her squirrel (she is allergic to cats) and we learn that Nigel, now on the run from Henry of Groswold, is William's son. William's house becomes a refuge for all and sundry whilst Nigel ends up building the courthouse that he had intended to destroy until, with all the characters assembled at William's house, Gwen's biscuits play a pivotal role in a final twist to the story.

Biscuits is a very well written one act play. The pace is perfect and the use of modern language adds humour to an already witty script.

BITCH BOXER
Author: Charlotte Josephine
Publisher: Oberon Modern Plays
ISBN NO: 9781849434775
Cast: 1F
Type: Full Length Monologue

The 2012 Olympics were the first to allow women to compete in the boxing ring. Here, hairbrush-in-the-mirror-karaoke and cherry sambuca loving, Chloe tells us of her journey to the fight of her life.

The day of her qualifier doesn't start well. She oversleeps then manages to lock herself out of the house when she goes out to put something in the bin. She has to go through a neighbour's house to get to the back garden and leap the fences to get to her own garden where she can shimmy up the drain pipe to her bedroom window. She can't get through the window; her "lady lumps" prevent it. However, she is able to hook her keys off the bedroom floor, retrace her steps and enter her house triumphantly through her front door just as her phone is ringing. She picks it up, full of herself, to hear two words: "Dad's dead".

It was Chloe's dad who started her boxing. When her mum left, with "some bloke she met in Tesco", Dad was devastated. He sat on the sofa crying for two weeks whilst Chloe smashed the house up. Then Dad got up and took Chloe down to the gym where she could channel that energy more constructively.

We reach a natural climax with the description of the qualifier which is every bit as exhilarating as we might expect. If Chloe is exhausted by then end of it then we are drained due to witnessing not only to the physical exertion, but also by the emotional journey she is forced to take during the fight.

As I was reading this monologue I was struck by how easily the words flew off the page, then I realised what the writer has done. The text has an airy rhythm to it and, without wishing to sound corny, it also delivers the odd punch. One might almost say that it floats like a butterfly and sings like a bee. Very clever: I suspect that there is much more to come from this talented young playwright.

BLUE SKY
Author: Clare Bayley
Publisher: Nick Hern Books
ISBN NO: 9781848423021
Cast: 2M 2F
Type: Full Length

Ray drives a roadside rescue truck for a living but the man who can is more interested in aeroplanes than cars. As the play begins he is at the perimeter fence of an isolated airport with an impressive range of photographic equipment. An old friend, Jane, appears. Her unexpected and improbable appearance is because she wants Ray's help tracing some information about an aircraft. Why she drove out to an isolated airport to see him rather than just drop round the next day is not explained.

Ray has a daughter, Ana, who was five the last time Jane saw her. She is now in her late teens and has ambitions to be journalist which is, coincidentally, Jane's profession. When they meet, however, they can hardly be said to have hit it off. Later Jane tells Ray what she wants. She has the tail number of an aeroplane that left Karachi where, according to reports, a suspected terrorist was bundled aboard a private aircraft. She wants to know if the tail number matches but Ray refuses to help. He doesn't want to get mixed up in that sort of thing.

Undeterred Jane uncovers more information including the details of a British man who disappeared after taking a flight to Pakistan. She interviews the man's wife but stories of disappearing planes, the CIA and 'outsourced torture' are too much to comprehend. The woman believes her husband has simply gone off with another woman. But Jane continues to piece things together and it becomes clear that the British government have been complicit in CIA operations and Ray's little isolated airport is all part of the underhand activity.

The subject of this play is potentially explosive, presenting evidence of Britain's involvement in acts that are both illegal and immoral in the name of the "war against terror", however, it doesn't work, mainly due to poorly conceived characters and unconvincing dialogue but also because not very much happens. The characters are not particularly engaging, their relationships seem unbelievable and the story just kind of peters out. All rather disappointing.

BLUE STOCKINGS
Author: Jessica Swale
Publisher: Nick Hern Books
ISBN NO: 9781848423299
Cast: 13M 8F
Type: Full Length

Girton College, Cambridge, was the first residential college in Britain for women. But, at the end of their studies, they were unable to obtain a degree and left the college merely as a Blue Stocking: an unqualified but educated woman. It is 1896 and we follow the story of Tess and her fellow students through their academic year as they fight for the right to graduate.

Their education begins with their tutor, the eccentric Mr Banks, inviting Tess to mount a bicycle (whilst he turns his back to preserve her modesty, naturally) in order to demonstrate Isaac Newton's theory of mechanics and the first law of motion: that an object will continue in its state of rest, known as inertia, until it is affected by an outside force, in this case Tess whom he instructs to press down on the pedal.

Once the lectures begin, things are as you might expect: the women raise their hands to answer a question but are ignored even though none of the men are able to give the answer; Tess perseveres and is ordered out of the lecture hall; the rest of the women are threatened with expulsion unless they learn their place. Our story, to date, has been rather pedestrian.

Of course with the advent of mixed education there is the distraction of the opposite sex and we also get what feels like quite a naive subplot of class divide where the woman from the poor background, the most brilliant student, is forced to return home to care for her family when her mother dies.

The remaining women continue their studies until, finally, the whole university has a vote on whether they should be allowed to graduate. They lose; it wasn't until 1948 that women were able to gain a degree from Cambridge University.

Blue Stockings is pleasant enough but, given the subject matter, I was hoping for rather more than an inoffensive Rom-Com and with a running time of around two hours, these stockings have a fair amount of unnecessary filler.

BORIS GODUNOV
Author: Adapted from the novel by Alexander Pushkin by Adrian Mitchell
Publisher: Oberon Books
ISBN NO: 9781849432559
Cast: 16M 7F
Type: Full Length

Russia in 1598. The Tsar, Ivan the Terrible, is dead and Boris Godunov is expected to take up the crown despite having locked himself in a monastery for the last month claiming that he has no desire to be Tsar. The evidence suggests otherwise. Why would Godunov have ordered the assassination of young Prince Dmitry if not to clear the way for his own ascendancy? In Red Square people plead with Boris. They wail, they cry (some with assistance from raw onions); they demand he be their Tsar. Finally, reluctantly, he agrees.

Ten years later and a young monk, Grigory, is persuaded to avenge the prince's death and pose as Dmitry to claim the crown. In the tavern on the Lithuanian border he meets a pair of travelling monks/drunks who provide some delightful comedy before Boris's guards arrive to arrest Grigory. Fortunately for him, he is the only one there capable of reading the arrest warrant and tricks the guards into arresting one of the drunk monks instead.

Rumour spreads that Dmitry survived and supporters clamour around Grigory believing him to be the true heir to the throne. But he is wise enough to know that the most powerful people in the world, popes and kings, do not care whether he is the resurrected Prince or a pretender; they see him as a catalyst for turmoil and someone who can be used to their advantage.

When Boris dies, his son Fyodor becomes the new Tsar but his reign is short lived. In Red Square the people wail and cry. They demand that Grigory (whom they believe to be Dmitry) be their Tzar. Finally, triumphantly, he agrees.

Adrian Mitchell's easy telling of this classic tale is joy from start to finish. Russian literature has a reputation for being unfathomable, but in Boris Godunov, Mitchell has stripped away the unnecessary and produced a coherent and, at times, very funny play that entertains as it educates; thus making it an excellent choice for school or youth theatre.

BOYS
Author: Ella Hickson
Publisher: Nick Hern Books
ISBN NO: 9781848422629
Cast: 4M 2F
Type: Full Length

Never judge a book by its cover is an idiom that I have taken to heart in my time reviewing scripts for Amateur Stage Magazine. So often I have picked up a script that doesn't look at all appealing from the blurb on the back only to find that the play within the covers moves and excites me. Such was the case with Precious Little Talent, a play by Ella Hickson, that I reviewed in these pages a while back, so when the award winning author's new play popped through my letterbox I was filled with anticipation.

Like Precious Little Talent, Boys is about young people setting out on life's journey. We are in the kitchen of a five man student flat in Edinburgh. There has been a party. Cam is asleep under the kitchen table still wearing the party hat that he had on last night. Benny enters. Despite the fact that, for reasons best known to himself, he positions himself on top of the fridge, we soon learn that Benny is the sensible one. He is followed into the kitchen by Timp; a party animal who proceeds to make a cup of tea for the severely hung-over Cam.

There is an air of expectancy as the boys reflect on the coming to the end of their student days, the end of the lease on the flat and, more pressing than that, the fact that in five hours time Cam is due to play lead violin in a televised concert. But first, Cam and Timp want to fill Benny in on what he missed during last night's party.

There was a girl: sixteen, maybe seventeen who got drunk and demanded sex. Mack, a fourth student tenant apparently obliged but, amongst all the male bravado, Benny wants to know if the girl was OK. Was there anyone there to look after her? Meanwhile, Cam has gone to the toilet and returns asking why there is a naked girl in the bath. The others are perplexed. It would be silly to have a bath with your clothes on, wouldn't it?

Later, a nervous and unwilling Cam is persuaded by Benny to go to his concert whilst the others contemplate how to get rid of all their rubbish. First, though, it is time for another party: one in which a girl named Laura covers her body with sushi on which, with chopsticks in her hair, ginger and wasabi in her palm and soy sauce in her belly button, she invites the boys to dine.

There are white vans outside which they imagine are council vans to collect the rubbish but, when a triumphant Cam returns, he tells them that there are police vans all the way down Princess Street. They must be expecting a demo or something. Then there is an explosion. With the riots of 2011 raging outside, the tension rises in the flat.

Throughout the play there is a constant theme: an empty chair that once belonged to Benny's brother who killed himself; his death perhaps a metaphor for their lives which the boys believe to be pointless. Provoked by Mack, there are arguments and a fight. Allegiances are formed and broken but as things begin to reach boiling point the students find they are all much too stoned to do anything anyway.

Did this script live up to expectations? The play is way too long but, having said that, I'd expect the majority of audience members would consider (watching) it a couple of hours well spent. With lots of adult humour to shock and amuse, the character's lives and aspirations are sufficiently interesting to hold our attention for the duration of the play. However, I don't imagine we are going to want to keep in touch with the boys. I'm not really interested in how their lives turn out: the story has no lasting impact and will be forgotten soon after leaving the theatre.

Whilst I found Boys a bit of a disappointment I am sure that there is plenty more to come from Ella Hickson and I look forward to reading more of her work in the future.

THE BRIDGE
Author: Gabe Torrens
Publisher: Drama Association of Wales
ISBN NO: 9781908575036
Cast: 2M 1F
Type: One Act

It is a dark and stormy night. Dave sits on a bridge sobbing, and sopping wet. After a moment he climbs over the railing and prepares to leap to his death in the water below. As he mutters, "I'm sorry", to himself a stranger approaches and asks him just-what-the-bloody-hell-he-thinks-he-is-doing.

This stranger is anything but sympathetic but he still encourages Dave to talk. He is, actually, anything but a stranger having been Dave's childhood friend, room-mate and Best Man. As they talk about their past we realise that something is amiss. Not only does it become clear that something has happened to change their relationship but there is something about the 'stranger' that makes him seem unreal.

Unfortunately, I believe that any audience will realise quite early on in the performance that the stranger is either a ghost or Dave's imagination and, although the reason why Dave finds himself in his current state of mind and the history that he shares with his friend makes for quite an interesting story, the anti-climax of having worked out the pair's relationship means that this play doesn't quite hit the mark.

BRIEF ENCOUNTERS
Author: Mark Robberts
Publisher: Lazy Bee Scripts
ISBN NO: None
Cast: 3M 1F
Type: One Act

Today is an exciting day for Frank and Ralph. The famous steam locomotive, the Tornado, is due to make a journey along the historic Stockton to Darlington railway and Frank's wife, Ethel, will be aboard it waving a red scarf as the train passes. The pair are standing on a railway footbridge with an impressive array of photographic equipment to capture the moment for posterity.

With them is Eddie, a young man with little interest in the forthcoming event, who only seems to be there because he owns a car and Frank and

Ralph needed a lift. Not even Frank's assertion that George Stephenson was Pamela Stephenson's grand daddy is enough to spark his interest but, when Frank gets a telephone call from Ethel to say that the train is running late, it is Eddie who is left looking after the equipment whilst the older men go to the pub.

Although I was a bit puzzled by the pair going off to the pub, even though they had just said that it was only 10am, this does mean that Eddie is now alone when Jean enters. She is quite a flirtatious woman who is also there to see the train pass. Inevitably it comes whilst Frank and Ralph are still in the pub and, as the smoke clears, we see soot on the faces of the young pair and lipstick on Eddie that provides evidence of their brief encounter.

The script has a very old fashioned feel to it and I wonder when it was written, but it rolls along quite nicely and the gentle humour and unusual setting give it a certain appeal.

BUILDING ON SAND
Author: Claire Booker
Publisher: www.bookerplays.co.uk
ISBN NO: None
Cast: 2M 3F
Type: Full Length

Building On Sand, also known as Last Tango in Littlehampton, is a comedy set at the English seaside. Richard and Juliette are on holiday with batty Aunt Dot and Richard's old school friend, Dan, together with his young French girlfriend, Berenice.

Dan has something of a way with the ladies. Not only do we see how he has managed to capture the heart of a very beautiful girlfriend half his age, but we also witness how he charms Dot in a way that leaves Richard and Juliette lost for words. This seems to give Richard an idea. His first marriage broke down when his wife was unfaithful and, though everything seems fine with Juliette, he is frightened it might happen again. He decides to put her to the test and enlists the help of his charming friend to see if she can be tempted to stray.

Surprisingly, he agrees, though his seduction technique is unusual to say the least. It seems to be working though and, as Dan and Juliette get to know each other a bit better, Aunt Dot gets hold of the wrong end of the stick and warns Richard not to throw his marriage away making a fool of himself with Berenice.

This is a well constructed script and, whilst Dot has some lovely lines, it is the developing relationship between Dan and Juliette that will keep the audience interested. Richard's foolishness is punished but it is satisfying to see that Dan also gets his comeuppance in the end.

BULLY BOY
Author: Sandi Toksvig
Publisher: Nick Hern Book
ISBN NO: 9781848422964
Cast: 2M
Type: Full Length

When I think of Sandi Toksvig I associate her with TV programmes such as QI or with The News Quiz on Radio 4. Her infectious laugh and sharp wit have made her a popular panellist and presenter, so it is difficult to imagine her sitting writing a play about the mental health of serving soldiers. However, Bully Boy is a very accomplished piece of writing with tremendous insight into the moral issues of military occupation.

The Bully Boys is the nickname for Eddie's unit. An unfortunate moniker, it is a reference to the unit's use of the phrase "bully for you", but it has taken on greater meaning now that Eddie is accused of murdering one of the locals. An eight year old boy, Omar, was thrown down a well and Eddie is reported to have been closest to him when it happened. Falklands veteran, Oscar, has been despatched to investigate.

There is an explosion: an Improvised Explosive Device that takes out the truck that The Bully Boys are travelling in. Eddie survives because he and Oscar are in a different truck from the others. Eddie is being kept apart from his colleagues so that they cannot corroborate on a story. Now there is no one for Eddie to corroborate with.

Back in the UK Eddie has a breakdown, beating up his girlfriend and going on the run. When he is found he is sent to the Priory for treatment before facing a court martial. Oscar is not sure that Eddie is fit to plead but tells us that nothing much has changed in one hundred years; it is the Priory now instead of prison, but which is better? More Falklands veterans have committed suicide than were killed in the conflict: both British and Argentinians.

The two become closer as the trial approaches and Toksvig skilfully introduces a lot of humour into the play alongside the exploration of what causes ordinary people to act in monstrous ways in extraordinary circumstances. By the end they are almost friends and we begin to imagine that things might turn out OK; but Toksvig doesn't let us off that easily.

This is not a gloomy play: there is a lot of light amongst the shade; but it is a realistic story and these things seldom have happy ending in real life. Toksvig has taken a very real situation, something that is in the news on a very regular basis, and has used it to create a very compelling drama.

CAGE OF IRON
Author: Douglas Fulthorpe
Publisher: Unpublished
Cast: 8M 3F
Type: Full Length

We are in the control room of a U999 somewhere in the North Atlantic. This German U-boat, the Cage of Iron referred to in the title of the play, had a major role in Germany's prominence at sea during the early part of the Second World War, but it is now 1943 and the tide has turned.

Cage of Iron is described as a satire. The characters are in fact caricatures of German officers in countless war films, although comedy German accents are reserved for lines requiring particular emphasis. Kapitan Stollen and Leutnant Schlange are at the periscope and – Gott im Himmel – they spot a British battleship. The Duke of Cornwall is so secret that not even the British know of its existence but another officer, Muller, enters and insists that that the vessel is a German battleship in disguise. Chaos ensues, Schlange accuses Muller of calling him a spy and Kapitan Stollen is required to stand in judgement. Meanwhile the battleship starts to torpedo their U-boat. Despite this, Muller convinces his captain that the battleship was German. He has good reason for wanting his captain to believe this because Leutnant Muller is a British spy.

Eighteen months later and a lot of water has flowed over the bridge. Again a battleship is spotted but this time the situation is reversed and it is Muller who insists that the ship is the Duke of Cornwall. Again he wins his argument and they fire on and sink the battleship. Muller has pulled of an enormous coup. He has sunk Germany's last battleship.

Cage of Iron has everything: battles at sea; stolen gold; espionage; even an enemy cat, and, at first, I was a little overwhelmed by the complexity of the story. This is something that would require a film director with Steven Spielberg's budget to do it justice, but then I realised how it would work on stage. The unnatural conversation as the characters carefully explain the plot is part of the comedy of the piece and this, combined with jokes about things that have not yet been invented and a little bit of word play that Ronnie Barker himself would have been pleased to have written, make for a play that has plenty of laughs. Where the author has excelled, though, is through giving all his characters personalities that surpass the caricatures that we see on the surface. As a result they earn our sympathy whatever side they happen to be representing.

Douglas Fulhorpe has sent this play to the magazine without information on how he might be contacted but I would suggest that any readers wishing to know more about this play ask to be put in touch with him through his publishers New Theatre Publications.

CHALET LINES
Author: Lee Mattinson
Publisher: Nick Hern Books
ISBN NO: 97818484822674
Cast: 5F
Type: Full Length

Butlins, Skegness: chalet No 12. Abigail arranges sticks of Juicy Fruit chewing gum to form a piano keyboard and launches into a verse of Elton John's Don't Let the Sun Go Down on Me. She quickly sweeps the chewing gum away when her sister Jolene enters and has the best opening line that I have read in a long time – but not one I can repeat in these pages.

These grown up sisters are at Butlins to celebrate their nana Barbara's 70th birthday. The family have come to Butlins, Skegness: chalet No 12, for their holiday every year since 1961 and Barbara is hoping for a lavish, if not very sophisticated, celebration. Barbara's daughter and mother to the two sisters, Loretta, is knocking back the Cava in an attempt to get the party started whilst they await the arrival of Barbara's other daughter, Paula. As the drink flows, everything starts to unravel. Old arguments are revived, tension builds and Abigail is not in a party mood. But this isn't Abigail's party. It is Barbara's party and it will not start for her until Paula arrives – if she ever arrives.

With humour that would make an ardent fan of Mrs Brown's Boys blush, Chalet Lines lurches from one lewd topic to the next. There is little to like about this dysfunctional family and the author has failed to create convincing characters with enough depth to make us wonder what heartache lies behind the viciousness. As a result, when we go back in time to Barbara's wedding day, I cannot imagine the audience having a lot of sympathy for her, even though she is clearly being forced into a marriage against her will.

There is a naivety to the script that raises questions about the author's understanding of his chosen subject, whilst the story feels like a collision of ideas rather than a journey. The climax comes when Abigail, the "normal" one, announces that she is leaving a husband that everyone thinks is perfect. She is the only one who seems to have got it together, but Abigail's marriage is over, and so is the play. To be brutally honest, I share her relief.

CHILDREN OF THE WOLF
Author: John Peacock
Publisher: Samuel French
ISBN NO: 9780573110702
Cast: 2M 2F + Voices
Ttpe: Full Length

It is Robin and Linda's 21st birthday. The twins were given up for adoption shortly after they were born but have now traced their biological mother and father and arranged a meeting. But as the play begins, in total darkness, we sense that this is not going to be a happy tale.

The first thing we see is Linda's face illuminated by her cigarette but then, after Robin arrives, they throw open the curtains to reveal a once grand but now rather dilapidated room. The tension is immense as they await their mother. We soon realise that Linda is the stronger of the pair but she is cruel and manipulative. She uses Robin's vulnerability to her advantage, but it is clear that she is also nervous about the forthcoming encounter.

Their mother, Helena, arrives. She has been lured to the house with the promise that she will meet the twins' father, Michael, whom she hasn't seen for years, but without the knowledge that Linda and Robin are her children. Linda enjoys telling her and the twins then taunt their mother with a lurid re-enactment of how she met Michael. Linda forces Michael to simulate a sexual act with their mother before she describes how Michael rejected her after the twins were born.

They were having an affair. Helena was engaged to another man and Michael was already married, but the affair ended after Helena forced Michael to make a choice between her or his wife. Now Linda tells her mother that Michael has to make another choice. She has begun an affair with him herself, with her own father, the purpose being to force him to choose again. He can come to the house today to meet Helena, but if he does Linda has told him that she will never see him again. There's another twist: if he doesn't arrive by 10am Linda will kill her mother. There is one more dramatic twist in this gruesome tale but I'll keep that to myself. Suffice to say the ending is as shocking as everything that comes before it.

This play was first performed in Ireland in 1971 before transferring to London. What is extraordinary is that from a quick search of the internet it doesn't look as if it has been performed since, and there is no evidence of it having been previously published. Quite why Samuel French have picked this up after more than forty years I cannot say but I'm glad that they have. It is real edge-of-the-seat stuff and, with a story that remains plausible despite it being so shocking, it will have an audience gripped from start to finish.

THE CHIMES
Author: Adapted by Derek Webb from the story by Charles Dickens
Publisher: New Theatre Publications
ISBN NO: 9781840948783
Cast: 4M 1F with doubling
Type: One Act

Reviews of Derek Webb's work have frequently appeared in these pages and I have become quite a fan of his festival ready, one act comedies. This adaptation is, therefore, something of a departure for him, though his trademark of naturally flowing style is still very much in evidence.

The Chimes was published one year after A Christmas Carol and is similar in many ways to Dickens' most celebrated work though, in this case, the main action takes place not on Christmas Eve, but on New Year's Eve and it is not the spirits of Christmas that speak to the main protagonist but the spirits of the chimes.

Toby Veck is a ticket porter who scrapes together a living running errands whilst trying to support his daughter, Meg. We begin with Toby trying to guess what delicacy Meg has in her basket: he lists a number of disgusting sounding foods before arriving at the correct answer. They are both delighted that she has managed to obtain the very best stewed tripe! A fitting food for a celebration as Meg has some news for her father: she is to be married.

Two very strong characters are Alderman Cute, a self important man who loves to put people down, and Sir Joseph Bowley, who claims to be "a friend to the poor" but is, in truth, just as bad as Cute. Toby allows himself to be influenced by these two, believing them when they say that some people are simply born bad. But, as Toby sleeps, he is visited by the spirits of the chimes who show him how things might be unless he learns life's most important lesson; that love is everything.

Derek Webb has done well to capture the atmosphere of Dickens' London in this short adaptation. The characters are very well defined and the moral of the story comes across very strongly. The Chimes would be a good choice for anyone looking for a seasonal production that is a little different from the norm.

THE COMPLAINT
Author: Nick Whitby
Publisher: Nick Hern Books
ISBN NO: 9871848422759
Cast: 2M 2F
Type: Full Length

Afra has raised a complaint and has been asked to come in to discuss it. The way her complaint is handled gives rise to another complaint which is investigated by the very person about whom Afra is complaining. This gives rise to yet another complaint. And so it goes on.

This is a Kafkaesque nightmare in reverse, as it is the protagonist, Afra, who throws the administration into chaos when they get tied up by their own red tape. However, things don't work out too well for Afra in the end when she is forced into compliance once the processing of her complaint involves torture and the use of a polygraph.

The author's comments in this script recommend that the 'openly comic' elements of the play should not be overplayed. No advice is given on how to play the hidden comedy. However, the baffling absurdity of Nick Whitby's latest work has a certain charm and, so long as one doesn't weigh oneself down too much by trying to work out what lies behind the surrealism, the experience is diverting enough.

DEATH IN HIGH HEELS

Author: Richard Harris
Publisher: Samuel French
ISBN NO: 9780573110948
Cast: 3M 7F
Type: Full Length

Fancy a costume drama? What better than a play set in a London fashion house in the 1930s? But we are not in the elegant shop; we are in the back room that is never seen by customers where the staff are eagerly awaiting to hear which of them is to be sent to run a new branch opening in France.

As the play begins we meet the candidates: there is Irene, the efficient but ultimately good natured senior sales lady, the cool and aloof Miss Gregory, Dorian, a fussy and self-important man who is in charge of the showroom, and Miss Doon who the office cleaner believes is the favourite after she 'accidentally' noticed that Miss Doon had a lunch appointment with the boss noted in his diary.

But we know from the title of the play that the story is not about career progression and before long we have a sign of how things are going to develop. One of the juniors, Rachel, has a stain on her hat. Irene suggests that she pops out to the chemist to buy some oxalic acid to clean it. This is a toxic substance that looks just like salt. Yes, I think we can see where we are headed!

Miss Gregory and Miss Doon apparently despise each other. To add to the intrigue the cleaner, known to all as 'Macaroni' has something on her mind. Dorian, too, despises Miss Gregory whilst Aileen, another of the juniors, has a secret that too many people know already. The suspects are lining up nicely and it isn't long before we have a victim. But it is Miss Doon rather than Miss Gregory who falls to the floor clutching her throat.

Two days later and the staff are assembled to face the systematic questioning of the CID. The precise attention to detail, as each of the suspects are asked to recall the events of the fateful day, helps us to review the evidence and soon our minds will be jumping to conclusions about just whodunit and why. Then, just as we begin to congratulate ourselves on working out that Miss Doon was not the intended victim, the story takes a few twists and turns before reaching quite a satisfying conclusion.

Death in High Heels is a good old fashioned thriller with a nice variety of roles that I am sure many societies will find perfect for the acting talent that they have available.

DIRTY BUSINESS
Author: Derek Webb
Publisher: New Theatre Publications
ISBN NO: 9781840948455
Cast: 1M 2F
Type: One Act

We are in the impressive office of one Roger Beasley at County Hall. Roger is a Head of Department at a County Council charged with making cuts to meet government spending targets. As the play begins, it is early evening. Josie is unenthusiastically going about her job of cleaning the office when Angela, a fellow cleaner, walks in.

The banter, or 'intra-team communication' as it is known in official council documents, reveals that, though the women may not be close friends, they have developed an easy-going camaraderie that means they can make mocking little jokes about each other without either taking offence. It is the sort of relationship that can easily become conspiratorial, either as partners in crime or against one another. And this sets us up very nicely for what is to come. When they find that their own jobs are under threat their most immediate thought is which one of them is to go. But once they stumble upon some evidence that the Head of Department is having an affair they join forces to launch an offensive against Roger Beasley.

Unfortunately, their attempt at blackmail goes disastrously wrong and, just when we think they might have got the upper hand after all, there is one final twist guaranteed to leave the audience with a smile on their faces.

There is plenty to amuse in this play. A running theme of malapropisms from Joyce provides plenty of laughs whilst Angela's line about them being 'horizontal cleaners' – they don't do vertical surfaces – had me laughing out loud.

Derek Webb consistently produces funny and highly accessible comedies and Dirty Business is perfect for a one act festival.

THE DISTRESSED TABLE
Author: Melville Lovatt
Publisher: New Theatre Publications
ISBN NO: 9781840949018
Cast: 1M 1F
Type: One Act

The distressed table occupies the centre space of Bernard's village furniture shop. Its unique look is obtained by the workers in the factory in Indonesia, where it is manufactured, by hitting it with hammers and chains. Christine likes the table but would prefer it if it were less distressed.

However, the potential purchase is just the platform on which Melville Lovatt serves this enjoyable tale of two people seeking a way to move on with their lives. Bernard's wife has left him though, for now, he will only admit that she is "away on business". Christine's husband is responsible for the only bit of scandal ever to have occurred in this sleepy village. He was a banker who was caught with his hand in the till and subsequently committed suicide whilst in prison.

Bernard knows the story, of course, but doesn't know that he was Christine's husband until she leaves him a card so he can contact her if there is any news on the table. He recognises the name and regrets joking with her about it on what might loosely be termed "a date". The two of them have developed an odd relationship: both of them more than willing to take offence at the slightest provocation, yet they are drawn to each other for reasons that they cannot explain. When the truth does finally come out it seems like they might be starting a new chapter in their lives that will bring them closer together.

In his notes Melville Lovatt advises that the settings might be suggested rather than constructed and I believe that this style of presentation would work best with this quite enigmatic play. We get just a glimpse into the lives of Bernard and Christine, the author wisely choosing to leave much of the story to our imagination thereby giving us plenty to talk about on the way home.

DUCKABILITY SOUTH OF RUNCORN
Author: Scott Marshall
Publisher: J Garnett Miller
ISBN NO: 9780853436874
Cast: 2M
Type: One Act

We are in the headmaster's study of a not very successful independent boys' school. The headmaster has sent for one of the junior masters, Ponsonby, to have a word with him. He cannot remember what the word is, and neither can Ponsonby, so, instead, he gives him a largely inaccurate summary of recent events at the school.

The headmaster has the manner of an absent minded sergeant major as he covers subjects such as an expedition one of the masters once arranged up north: way up north – beyond Harrow, and the tragic death of another of the masters during a school cricket match. The tragedy being that, as a result of the mistimed death, they lost the match by three runs.

Finally we get the question of 'duckability'. There are two types of people in this world: eagles and ducks. A duck can no more become an eagle than an eagle can assume duckness. Ponsonby must decide which he is: a duck or an eagle.

He displays signs of being an eagle. His suggestion that Miss Dell, the stone deaf postmistress, should take over the vacant post of Head of Music shows that he is on the same wavelength as his headmaster. The same cannot be said for another master,: Smathering-Browne who has suffered a nervous breakdown after some of the pupils put live rats in his bed. Once the headmaster is finished with Ponsonby, Smathering-Browne is shown in. Convenient really, because Ponsonby and Smathering-Browne are played by the same actor.

The play ends with confusion and blackout as all three characters are on stage at the same time but I found the ending to be a bit weak after all the clever wordplay that had gone before it.

One note on the script itself: on some occasions the character names are abbreviated. At first I thought this was a typographical error but it occurs so frequently I think it must be to save space. It is rather distracting and I recommend that J Garnet Miller refrain from this practice in future.

DUSK RINGS A BELL

Author: Stephen Belber
Publisher: Nick Hern Books
ISBN NO: 9781848422018
Cast: 1M 1F
Type: Full Length

The play begins with a monologue. Molly tells us of her life: how she was born to hippy parents, how she got rid of her childhood stutter and just what she used to do in her bedroom whilst listening to The Smiths. She is interrupted in her flow by Ray who also starts to address the audience and between them, but unheard by one another, they set the scene.

Twenty four years ago Molly wrote herself a note setting out the course that she expected her life would take. Now she has returned to the house where she hid the note and retrieved it in order to compare how things have turned out to what she had anticipated. In order to get to the note she had to break a window and this explains the appearance of Ray who was, he says, called in by one of the neighbours. Molly thinks that she recognises him.

Gradually memories of a pair of teenagers kissing on the lifeboat stand, down at the beach, lead them to share their memories of growing up. They go for a coffee and seem to be getting on fine until Ray gets to the part where he has to explain why he became a caretaker rather than the heart surgeon he thought he would become. Two years after that night on the lifeboat stand Ray was involved in the murder of a young gay man and subsequently served ten years in prison.

Horrified by this crime, Molly leaves but arranges to meet Ray again a couple of weeks later. As she makes Ray talk about what happened she realises that it isn't only Ray who has to accept responsibility for what happens in life.

There is very little action in this play, mainly the pair just sit and talk, so it is important that the audience care about the characters otherwise they will lose interest very quickly. The text is there but I believe it would take two very strong performances to carry it off.

EATING THE LINO
Author: Scott Marshall
Publisher: J Garnett Miller
ISBN NO: 9780853436881
Cast: 2M 2F
Type: One Act

Eating the Lino is a one act play for two couples in their seventies. They are enjoying a nightcap in the shabby lounge of their holiday home when Len starts to tell the others about a story he has read in the newspaper (sounds like the Daily Mail to me) about how money that we send to poor third world countries all ends up with an arms dealer in Russia.

This kick starts a wide ranging conversation that takes in the price of petrol, wonky supermarket trolleys, how much you have to multiply a dog's age by to get its age if it were human, ditto for rabbits, then onto vegetarians, one legged footballers and an old man who was apparently discovered by Social Services eating the lino in his caravan.

Eventually the topic turns to childhood memories and, once the men are on their own, the conversation becomes less light hearted as we learn that Len had an older sister, Edith, who was killed during the war. We are reminded that we all spend a great deal of our time talking about rubbish, possibly because the important stuff is too painful, and isn't long before we are back to nonsense about greenhouses and bus routes.

Eating the Lino is a gentle comedy with a few poignant moments and four excellent roles for older actors.

EGUSI SOUP
Author: Janice Okuh
Publisher: Nick Hern Books
ISBN NO: 987184842711
Cast: 2M 3F
Type: Full Length

Mrs Anyia is sitting on a suitcase in an attempt to get it closed. Her daughter, Grace, is telling her that she will have to take something out – leave something behind. "What can we leave?" asks Mrs Anyia, "The flowers? Allow your father to lie in a bare grave?" You see, the Anyia's are packing for a trip to Nigeria to attend a memorial service for John, Mrs Anyia's husband, who died a year ago.

The items that Mrs Anyia deem essential for her trip, which include a car steering wheel and an electricity generator, provide much comedy in the opening moments of what promises to be a warm, family play. Soon the other daughter, Anne, arrives from New York where she is "the big barristah" bringing with her gifts indicative of her relative wealth, but without the one thing her mother was hoping for she might bring with her – a husband.

As a family friend, Pastor Emmanuel from the Celestial Church of Christ, prays for Anne that she might find a good man in Nigeria whilst they are there, we see the differences in the life that Anne now leads compared to that of her family back in England.

This clash of cultures is the theme that runs through the play. Pastor Emmanuel declares that a woman without a man is like Egusi Soup without the egusi and, as egusi is a type of seed, this could be a declaration of, not only his opinion of women, but also his intentions towards Mrs Anyia.

In many ways this play is quite a traditional comedy. We get the warmth promised in the early scenes tempered with the conflict the clash of cultures but, whilst I found Egusi Soup reasonably satisfying, I could have done with more spice.

EMILY DAVIDSON – DEEDS NOT WORDS
Author: Mitchell Doyle
Publisher: Unpublished
Contact: Via Amateur Stage Magazine
Cast: 4M 5F
Type: Short Three Act

Emily Davidson, you may remember, is the suffragette who was killed when she fell in front of the King's horse at Epsom in 1913. The play begins, however, in 1979. The country is facing a general election; a choice between Jim Callaghan and Margaret Thatcher. Kitty Blanshaw, a local newspaper reporter, interviews Matilda Huntington-Green, a woman who was present when Lady Astor, the first female Member of Parliament, was elected in 1929.

However Matilda's reminiscences take us back to 1913 when, as a young woman, she was totally against the idea of votes for women. She thought it best left to the men who had had the necessary education. We might be expecting to learn how Emily Davidson changed her mind, but that is not how the story goes. In fact, Matilda believes that Emily's act was a stunt that set the women's movement back and it might have never succeeded without the First World War. It was the fact that men could make such foolish decisions that resulted in millions losing their lives that changed the mind of Matilda and many like her.

I enjoyed Matilda the elder's commentary on the events from earlier in her life and it was pleasing that the play ends with a fact that was unknown to me. However, I do think that the author has tried to cram too much into a relatively short play. The opening scene gives us a good flavour of how things were in 1979 compared to the present day and one hundred years ago, but it also overcomplicates the plot. Nevertheless, I enjoyed reading this script and admire the educational value.

ENTERTAINING ANGELS
Author: Alistair Ferguson
Publisher: Unpublished
Contact: www.aapantos.co.uk
Cast: Variable. Min 10 plus chorus
Type: Full Length

Entertaining Angels, described as a Christmas Entertainment, is a morality tale for the modern world. Set in a travelling circus, a stranger informs us that she has been sent by 'the boss' to sort out the whole sorry mess. On the verge of bankruptcy, The Jongleur's Travelling Circus is looking somewhat shabby. Furthermore, the latest idea for bringing in some extra trade – a circus nativity – does not meet with all round approval. The stranger is there to help, but she has a rival. If the stranger represents good then Lilleth represents, well, the other.

Meanwhile Mike, who runs the circus, has a daughter, Mary, who tells her father that she has 'met someone' and intends to marry him. This is a problem for Mike because he believes that circus people should marry circus people; the person that Mary wants to wed is not a circus person. He is a carpenter by the name of Joe.

With much of the text in verse, the author has obviously put a good deal of effort into producing a script that is literate, well planned and brimming with good ideas. Unfortunately, I am struggling to imagine who the audience would be for this play. It would go over the heads of most children and, although there is a stage direction near the end to encourage the audience to join in with a dance, I don't believe that the play would produce the kind of atmosphere where this would be possible. This is a pity. It's a good script but I feel it just needs more gaity.

FALSE PRETENCES
Author: Eric Chappell
Publisher: Samuel French
ISBN NO: 9781573111259
CAST: 5M 2F
TYPE Full Length

The Bounder was a short lived television series in the early nineteen eighties starring Peter Bowles of To The Manor Born fame. He played Victor, a none too successful con artist recently released from prison in a comedy that relied upon the actor's persona as much as it did on the script. This play is the writer's own adaptation for the stage.

The situation is quickly established. Kevin is a respectable estate agent, living in a respectable house with his respectable wife, Valerie. Her recently widowed friend, Lucy, is staying with them when her less than respectable brother, Victor, arrives having completed his two year jail term.

On first appearance prison seems to have taken a toll. Victor is pale, withdrawn and walks with a stick. He is not half the man he used to be. Except that he is – once a con artist, always a con artist and, although Kevin is perfectly aware of this, he is too polite to throw his brother-in-law into the street.

Victor sets about wooing Lucy. He is after her money, of course, but his plans go awry. She was supposed to have refused the expensive bracelet that he got on approval from the jeweller's but, instead, she graciously accepted despite his attempts to get her to throw it back in his face. On a more positive note, he has persuaded the bank manager to advance him a loan on the strength of a map of Africa showing the location of a secret diamond mine. But the 'uncut diamonds' Victor has from the mine are made from washing powder and the bank manager and the jeweller are friends.

The arrival of Soapy Simpson, a cell mate of Victor's posing as an artist, affords us an opportunity for a bit of humour about the ladies being painted in the nude and we feel like we are in very familiar territory by the time we reach the conclusion and find that the only person Victor was fooling was himself.

The release of this script is no doubt prompted by the success of the stage version of the writer's more celebrated sitcom, Rising Damp, but I suspect that False Pretences would have felt dated thirty years ago, never mind now, and it is difficult to see how a play like this has much relevance to audiences today.

FATHER'S DAY
Author: Allan Williams
Publisher: Drama Association of Wales
ISBN NO: 9781898740988
Cast: 2M 1F
Type: One Act

Ginger Harris is an old man who sits in an armchair whilst his daughter, Alice, finishes off the housework. Her visits, she admits, are infrequent at the best of times and this will be the last one before going away for three weeks leaving her father to cope on his own.

A quick peck on the cheek and she is gone but before long Harris has another visitor: a young man by the name of Jamie who claims to be from the gas board. It isn't long before our suspicions about Jamie are confirmed and he is demanding to know where Harris keeps his money. But he underestimates the old man and is knocked unconscious when he turns his back.

Coming round, Jamie finds himself tied to a chair and forced to listen to Harris's life story. He begs the old man to call the police but Harris is determined to get retribution for all the injustices he has suffered throughout his long life.

The short scene with Alice at the beginning seems a bit forced and would be unnecessary except that it establishes that she is his only regular visitor. This makes for a nice twist at the end but I feel that we didn't really get to know Harris and Jamie well enough to care what happens to them.

A FINE BRIGHT DAY TODAY
Author: Philip Goulding
Publisher: Samuel French
ISBN NO: 9780573111327
Cast: 1M 2F
Type: Full Length

Margaret and her daughter Rebecca live in a seaside cottage on England's south coast. Margaret's husband died thirty years ago, when Rebecca was still a baby, and they have lived quite an isolated life ever since with few visitors to the house, though they do both work and Rebecca has half moved out to live with her boyfriend. As the play begins she is finally moving out for good and there is a very cool atmosphere between mother and daughter as the boyfriend sits outside in the van waiting for the last of the boxes.

Meanwhile, Milton, an American visiting the sea to paint the landscape, needs somewhere to lodge. Rebecca meets him in a pub and suggests that he could stay with her mother. When she passed this information on to Margaret, during a breezy visit with forced cheerfulness and a desperate need to give her mother the news and leave, she makes the excuse that she'd had a few pints and her judgement was not what it should be. A stunned Margaret asks what she is supposed to say to Milton, should he turn up. Rebecca tells her not to worry. When he meets Margaret, Rebecca is doubtful that Milton will want to stay.

But stay he does. Margaret and Milton make an odd couple, but perhaps that is to their advantage. Neither of them goes in for social niceties all that much but they are also both slow to take offence. As it happens, they get along just fine. In fact, for someone who hasn't had another man in the house for thirty years, Margaret seems a little too comfortable; despite all her talk about being awkward and unused to company she seems to find talking to Milton quite easy. In a scene where the pair of them get gently tipsy, their shame that they are actually having fun is both charming and sad.

In truth, it is quite an unlikely story but that is largely irrelevant because the characters are totally believable, helped by some quirky dialogue: Rebecca is cutting out caffeine "on account of her heads"; Daily Mail reading Margaret believes that "Seventy-five percent of all fatalities are due to domestic appliances. The rest are down to foreign intervention."

A Fine Bright Day Today is essentially a love story and when Rebecca asks if Milton is sleeping with her mother his response is to ask if it is any of her business. She replies that she doesn't want her mother to get hurt. But neither does he and, by the end, Milton and Margaret have forced their way into our hearts so much that we are desperate for a happy ending. I'm happy to say that we get it.

FIRST EPISODE
Author: Terence Rattigan and Philip Heimann
Publisher: Nick Hern Books
ISBN NO: 9781848421639
Cast: 6M 2F
Type: Full Length

First Episode is Terrence Rattigan's first play which made its début at a small experimental theatre in Kew in 1933 when Rattigan was just 22. It transferred to the West End and then on to New York. Despite the overnight success, the critics didn't like it and it has never been revived. It is now published for the first time to mark the centenary of the author's birth.

Written in collaboration with Philip Heimann, whilst Rattigan was still a student, we have here the story of a love triangle featuring a pair of undergraduates and an older woman. The university drama company is staging a production of Anthony and Cleopatra and the director, Tony, has managed to persuade a professional actress, Margot, to appear in the play. His motives, however, go beyond a mere appreciation of her talent. He is infatuated with her and overjoyed that she has accepted his invitation.

Tony shares a house with three others: Bertie a rather immature young man, Philip an older and wiser person and David, who behaves like a bit of a cad. At a party after a rehearsal Margot is invited to join the others but soon after she arrives it is time for her to go. Members of the opposite sex are not permitted after midnight but Tony makes a secret pact with Margot and, somewhat surprisingly, she returns via a window once Tony is alone. Although we get the impression that he is quite experienced around women, he is obviously totally smitten with Margot and he declares his love for her.

Two weeks later, the production is at an end and Margot is due to return to town, but Tony is having none of it. On a sudden impulse they go away together for the weekend, much to David's dismay. David is the third component of this love triangle but he has no affection for Margot. Indeed, his attitude toward her is bordering on hostile and he is relieved, some time later after a number of weekends away, when Tony admits that he had mistaken his feelings for Margot. It was only infatuation after all, but now he finds himself unable to get rid of her.

David's concern throughout has been for the well being of his friend but his efforts in preventing him from being hurt result in unfortunate consequences for both himself and Margot but, as he reflects at the end of it all, they were just two unlucky people in Tony's first episode.

I am not surprised at the instant success of this play. Although there are signs of Rattigan's immaturity as a writer, for example the characters seem a little clichéd, the risqué storyline must have been a real attention grabber at the time. It is not, however, his finest work and I feel the publication is really only of academic interest.

FIT TO DROP
Author: John Waterhouse
Publisher: New Playwrights Network
ISBN NO: 9870861394818
Cast: 1M 3F
Type: One Act

One thing that a theatre audience has to accept when watching a play is the rather unnatural spectacle of the characters speaking to each other without facing each other. Unless the play is performed in the round they will usually be required to face the fourth wall and somehow make this look natural. However, there are a few plays where facing the fourth wall is natural and the setting of this one, a gym (or fitness centre as they seem to be called these days), is an excellent example. Three running machines are lined up perfectly so that the main characters are ideally placed to project their lines directly into the auditorium. (How the theatre procures three running machines is another matter).

The exercising ladies are: Dora, an active pensioner who fantasises about murdering her husband of forty years; Julia, a middle aged woman bored with her life; and Emma, a young woman who divorced her husband after he ran off with the postman. She now has an eye on Brian, an instructor who, unfortunately for Emma, is married to the manager of the gym.

49

The dialogue is rather unsubtle but it probably needs to be in a play that packs so much story into a running time of only about fifteen minutes. Whilst there is a small amount of fairly sophisticated word play, most of the laughs are of the easy variety; such as Emma naming her child Tarquin. The characters are quite two dimensional which is disappointing with an author as experienced as John Waterhouse. I wonder if he might have done better if he had cut out some of the action or expanded the characters by making the play longer.

FLEABAG
Author: Phoebe Waller-Bridge
Publisher: Nick Hern Books
ISBN NO: 9781848423640
Cast: 1F
Type: Full Length

I hesitate to describe this as a monologue because there are a number of characters in this play even if Fleabag is the only one on stage. The other characters' lines can either be pre-recorded or spoken by the actress. It begins with a job interview which goes horribly wrong when Fleabag goes to remove her jumper forgetting that she is not wearing a top underneath. The interviewer thinks that he is being propositioned and the interview soon turns into a slanging match.

The reason that Fleabag is looking for a job is because she is skint. She runs a café that she started with her friend, Boo, but now Boo is dead: she walked into a cycle lane hoping for an injury that would land her in hospital and teach her boyfriend a lesson, but three people died in the resulting accident. Now hardly anyone comes into the café leaving Fleabag plenty of time to think about sex; which she does just about all the time.

Fleabag puts it best herself: "I have a horrible feeling I'm a greedy, perverted, selfish, apathetic, badly dressed, cynical, depraved, mannish-looking, morally bankrupt woman". Her dad's response is that she must get all that from her mother.

To say that the humour is adult oriented would be the understatement of the year; it is absolutely filthy. But, if you can accept the rudeness, then it is also very funny and there is pathos by the bucket load. Fleabag has a habit of destroying things, most commonly she destroys the things that are important to her, but any sympathy we may feel for her is countered by a sense that she deserves everything that happens to her; her addiction to sex more important to her than friends and family.

This is a play that will divide people due to the adult content, but there is no doubting the writer's talent.

FOXFINDER
Author: Dawn King
Publisher: Nick Hern Books
ISBN NO: 9781848422445
Cast: 2M 2F
Type: Full Length

William Bloor is a fox finder. He has written to Samuel and Judith to tell them that he will be staying at their farmhouse whilst he investigates the area for contamination. They are perplexed. Why them? And his attitude when he arrives is curious to say the least: he refuses to enter the house until they have provided evidence of their identity.

After dinner he questions them about wild animals seen in the area. He is methodical in his work. It is wartime and this farm is failing to produce the required quota set by the government. He is there to help, he says.

Next morning and a neighbour, Sarah, calls in with a pamphlet she was given in the town which proclaims that foxes are our friends. Judith hides it, knowing that if William sees the literature it will mean trouble. She is clearly worried by his presence and there follows an excruciating scene where she is questioned by him with embarrassing thoroughness about her sexual relations with Samuel.

As the play develops we realise that the fox is a metaphor. Sarah's distribution of the pamphlet led to her being classed by William as a collaborator, and this term is also applied to Samuel and Judith when they deny that there are foxes on their farm. The fox represents all that is evil and William insists that it is because the farm is contaminated that the couple have had such a bad run of things: the accidental death of their son, poor health and failing crops are all, according to William, due to the presence of 'the beast'.

Foxfinder is an entertaining, if somewhat bleak, play with easily identifiable characters and a sense of other worldliness that will give an audience plenty to ponder after the curtain has fallen.

FUTURE SHOCK
Author: Richard Stockwell
Publisher: Drama Association of Wales
ISBN NO: 9781898740995
Cast: 1M 2F
Type: One Act

Laura wakes up feeling nauseous. She sits on the side of her bed as Nicoletta enters wearing clothes that suggest she is a medical practitioner. She doesn't have much of a bedside manner, however, and coldly refuses to answer most of Laura's questions.

Gradually we become aware that Laura hasn't just woken up but has, in fact, been revived following a long period of suspension. She was considered worthy of preservation in 'her time' but now, centuries later, standards have changed, her slightly bruised toe being a blemish considered unacceptable in this day and age.

We find that Laura has been revived early, before the planned re-union with her partner (who is away on a mission) because the trust that was paying for her suspension has run out of funds. Now she will have to live out the rest of her life and be long dead by the time her partner returns.

There is an alternative. Laura's legal representative suggests creating a digital image that records everything there is of Laura, right down to her bruised toe. From this, she can be re-created for her partner at the appropriate time. There is just one condition. To avoid any possibility of two Laura's existing at the same time, if she is to accept this proposal she must also accept her immediate death.

I have to be honest and say that science fiction is not really my bag. I tend to be distracted by what I see as inconsistencies in the author's vision of the future. For example, in this story Nicoletta has a telephone implanted in her head which she controls with her eyes. Fair enough, but why then does she have to cart around a cumbersome electronic notebook? Surely she would be able to consult some futuristic version of Wikipedia by wiggling her ears.

But I am being flippant; Future Shock could make an interesting piece of theatre. The tension between the nurse type character and the legal representative keeps us interested and Laura's decision to make the ultimate sacrifice due to that old fashioned concept – love – give the script a nice sense of humanity in an alien world.

THE GATEKEEPER

Author: Chloe Moss
Publisher: Nick Hern Books
ISBN NO: 9781848422605
Cast: 2M 3F
Type: Full Length

A holiday cottage in the Lake District and Mike and Julia are hiding behind the sofa. They arrived early and Julia thought it would be fun to leap up and surprise their daughter when she arrives. Unfortunately, when she does so, Stacey is on her mobile phone shouting and swearing at someone from work. The surprise goes a little flat.

These opening moments of the play give us a good indication of what we are in for. Here we have a family struggling to connect when they are not quite on the same wavelength. Things seem to be going well for Stacey, though. She has a good job and her partner has just had a huge bonus. Why then does she want to borrow money from her father?

Stacey is not the only one with a secret. Meet Rob, Stacey's brother, who has arrived with his girlfriend, Angela. Rob has been in prison, but only Stacey knows this. The others believe his story that he has been living in Thailand. He even arranged for postcards to be sent from that country whilst he was inside. At least he paid another inmate to arrange this, but it seems that he has been taken for a ride.

With everyone together, there follow some excruciating party games which we know will end in tears. The drink flows, tongues are loosened and, eventually, fists fly as the family gathering disintegrates into miserable chaos.

The Gatekeeper is a darkly comic tale of a family who can hardly be bothered to keep up the pretence any more. It is a bit on the long side, and would certainly benefit from a few trims, but the tension builds nicely to an explosive climax.

GETTING DARK
Author: Joe Graham
Publisher: J Garnett Miller
ISBN NO: 9780853436607
Cast: 1M 2F
Type: One Act

Getting Dark is a dramatisation of The Ribbon of Truth by Kal Gibson. This is the true story of a girl's descent into blindness. In Joe Graham's astonishing play the story is narrated by Karen who, now an adult, relives her terrifying experiences of childhood.

As a six year old Karen wants the light on when she is in bed. She insists that this is not because she is frightened of the dark despite the night time stories her father tells her about trolls; she just cannot sleep unless the light is on. At school she is regarded as clumsy. The other children tease her and hide her things, knowing that she will have trouble finding them. She once went home in someone else's coat because it had been put on her peg. Her mother called her stupid. But now she must sleep because she has a big day tomorrow.

The next day she has a visitor. It is Easter and Mr Marks has brought Karen a large chocolate egg wrapped in a yellow ribbon. He is the headmaster at a specialist blind school and her mother explains that he has come to have a chat about Karen going there to board. "Oh, the blind thing," says Karen. Her parents have told her that she is going blind but it is all very bewildering. Does going to a blind school make you go blind? Do glass eyes help you to see?

Karen is a very frightened little girl and most of her fear comes from not understanding what is happening to her. On the surface her parents seem distant and unkind. One would expect them to have more sympathy, more perception of the fears their daughter faces, but this is not a one sided story. Karen is shown to be a difficult and demanding six year old. Her parents are having to cope with a new baby in the house as well as coming to terms with their daughter's onset of blindness, but things said in the heat of the moment can remain with one for life. Karen was not afraid of the dark. She did not believe in bogeymen; but, as the play draws to a close with her lying in bed in the dormitory at her new school, she does now.

Getting Dark pulls at the heartstrings without being sentimental. Thought provoking and moving it provides an actress with an opportunity to excel in a challenging but rewarding role in a play that would make an excellent choice for a festival.

GIRLS LIKE THAT

Author: Evan Placey
Publisher: Nick Hern Books
ISBN NO: 9781848423534
Cast: 6-24F
Type: Full Length

When a naked photograph of her goes viral on the internet, Scarlett is suddenly the centre of attention for all the wrong reasons. Everyone who knows her has something to say but Scarlett herself is keeping her mouth shut. To understand how we got here we go back in time to when Scarlett and the other girls are five years old and enter the St. Helen's School for Girls. This is a school that selects just 20 girls each year based on their academic ability and their potential to think outside the box. For example: "Sophie has a car with only one working door. She has five friends who each take 45 seconds to enter through the door and take their seat. How many of them will be seated 90 seconds after Sophie unlocks the door?" Answer: "All of them. It's a convertible".

For the next seven years these girls progress through their education. Always together; always in the same class. They are like a family; but they have a pecking order, just like the chickens on one girl's farm. Scarlett is at the bottom. At secondary school the girls are still together, not listening to their history teacher talking about "suffering jets", when their mobile phones all go off. Each of them has received a photo message. Every one the same. A photo of Scarlett. Naked. Some press delete, others press forward. Within the minutes the whole school has it.

Later the phones receive another naked photo but this one is not Scarlett; it is Russell, the school hunk. Where Scarlett was a slut, Russell is a hero. Boys high five him in the corridor. Everyone assumes that Scarlett and Russell took the photos of each other and Scarlett is beaten up by Russell's girlfriend. Scarlett transfers to another school but the photo is soon doing the rounds there and suddenly the police are asking questions. Scarlett has gone missing; the girls fear suicide.

All of the lines in this script are spoken directly to the audience, never to each other, and the majority of them are not assigned to any particular character. This gives the play a sense of detachment reflected on the script cover which has lines from the play as they might appear on a social media website. The problem, for me, is that it seems as though it is trying too hard to appeal to a teenage audience. It is full of issues that face young people whilst growing up but doesn't offer any solutions and the style of delivery gives it a feel of being a step away from reality. All of which means that Evan Placey's play, like his character, Scarlett, is likely to face rejection.

THE GOD OF SOHO
Author: Chris Hannan
Publisher: Nick Hern Books
ISBN NO: 9781848421684
Cast: 6M 5F
Type: Full Length

In heaven the Gods are discontent: Big God's daughter, Clem, has been rejected by her lover, The New God, who finds her palatable when clothed but utterly repulsive when naked. He clearly has unconventional tastes, but rejection means that Clem must be banished to earth.

Meanwhile in Soho, Baz, a rock musician, and Joe, an actor, are snorting cocaine on the rooftop of a nightclub. Some bouncers and a policewoman appear. The latter asks Joe for his autograph. The bouncers ask Baz to leave.

Next we meet Natty, a reality TV star who hates her own life and whose volatile relationship with Baz has reached breaking point. Then we find ourselves in Kings Cross where Clem is surrounded by pimps, sex workers, their punters, Dog People in collars and their owners. All this and we are only twelve pages into the script!

So what is the play about? I suppose it is a love story of sorts: how that most peculiar emotion can be both devastating and joyful and how nobody is immune to it, no matter how wild and unconventional their lifestyle. Even Natty and Baz are forced, in the end, to let nature take its course.

I was going to describe this play as a roller-coaster but that would be inaccurate. It is more of bucking bronco: out of control, heaving and swirling, leaving us nauseous from the non-stop filth and unpleasantness of it all. Once unseated, few of us would want to get back on.

GOODBYE TO ALL THAT

Author: Luke Norris
Publisher: Nick Hern Books
ISBN NO: 9781848422599
Cast: 2M 2F
Type: Full Length

David has just picked up his A level results and has gone to his grandad's golf club to give him the news. His grandad, Frank, enters having just completed a round with his pal, Mike, except that David knows this not to be true. For one thing, he has just seen Mike at the school and, for another, he has just seen his grandad holding hands with a woman who is not his grandma. Frank, sixty-nine years old and married to Iris for forty-five years, is having an affair.

Her name is Rita. Three years ago, for the first time in his life, Frank fell in love. Being found out has brought Frank to his senses; he cannot continue with the deception, he is going home to leave Iris.

He does just that. He tells her that he doesn't love her. He tells her about Rita. Then he goes back to the golf club to get very drunk. Later he returns home to collect a suitcase but he is incapable of doing anything. Considering the circumstances Iris is quite tolerant, she even puts a pair of pyjama bottoms on her husband and tells him to stay the night. She thinks he is just drunk – doesn't realise that he is having a stroke.

David goes to visit Rita. He is angry and acts immaturely. He is upset and wants someone to blame, but he is to provide the link between Rita and his granddad. Frank survives the stroke but needs constant care. He is placed in a miserable NHS care home but Rita has money and can pay for him to go private. Eventually Iris gives up the man she loves but who never loved her, but it is too late for him to enjoy the life with Rita that he had planned.

Goodbye to All That is a tender play with some good elements. I like the way that David is forced to grow up and take responsibility even though it leads to conflict with his grandma. Of the four characters Rita is one who seems a bit two dimensional but it is pleasing to read a script from a young writer with good parts for older actors.

GREAT EXPECTATIONS
Author: Adapted by Jo Clifford from the novel by Charles Dickens
Publisher: Nick Hern Books
ISBN NO: 9781848420670
Cast: 10M 5F
Type: Full Length

Here we have another Dickens adaptation, the publication of which
is timed to cash in, sorry, respond to, increased interest in the author
on the bicentenary of his birth. However, Jo Clifford's adaptation of
Great Expectations differs from the others, that have dropped through
my letterbox in the last couple of years, in two ways. Firstly, it is by Jo
Clifford, a playwright who first came to my attention when she unjustly
attacked a play written by a friend of mine having never read nor seen
it. Secondly, this particular work has an honourable history. It was
first performed in 1988 after Clifford used Dickens' text to create an
experiment in dance and spoken word to a largely illiterate audience
and was revived as a stage play to tour the UK with an all star cast in
2012.

The story begins as Pip starts a journey to unravel the mysteries of
his past. From a "wretched, snivelling boy" he becomes a gentleman
through a series of unexpected turns and an unknown benefactor, but
the truth behind Pip's change in fortune is not what he expects.

Pip's desire to be a gentleman is, to some extent, driven by his attraction
to Estella, the beautiful but cold-hearted ward of the mysterious Miss
Haversham. The unexpected arrival of a lawyer changes Pip's life. A
person, whose identity must remain a profound secret, has instructed
that Pip is to be taken from his current humble sphere of life and be
made a gentleman: wealth and property is to be his inheritance.

Pip discovers that the lawyer acts for Miss Haversham and concludes
that she must be the mystery benefactor. This results in his becoming
somewhat arrogant, with a belief that certain things are pre-determined,
but when Estella marries Bentley Drummle, he learns that not
everything is to be handed to him on a plate. When Pip finally discovers
the true identity of his benefactor he realises that he had made a number
of incorrect assumptions about the people he had known.

Jo Clifford has demonstrated a lot of skill in preserving all the essential
elements of the story in a ninety minute stage play. Inevitably a lot

of background is omitted but she makes up for this with strong characterisation and simple story telling. For example, Pip's immediate appraisal of Bentley Drummle as a "rich, ugly brute" is believed because of the conviction with which it is stated. We are less sure that Pip is correct in his classification of others, Magwitch in particular, because the author is more enigmatic in the description of these characters. This all makes for a story that flows nicely and will be easily understood by audiences of all ages.

HALCYON DAYS
Author: Deirdre Kinahan
Publisher: Nick Hern Books
ISBN NO: 9781842423015
Cast: 1M 1F
Type: Full Length

We are in the conservatory of a nursing home in Dublin. Sean, 72, sits alone with his thoughts. He is still alone when Patricia enters because, though she chats away, Sean doesn't even acknowledge her existence. Not until he hears the tea trolley and this seems to bring him to life.

Patricia is a few years younger than Sean and is quite a feisty woman who has retained her appetite for good looking men. She thinks that she has heard of Sean. The two go round the houses for a while, trying to think of any mutual friends that they could have, before Sean reveals that he is an actor and has appeared in many films. Patricia googles him at her first opportunity.

Over time we witness a burgeoning relationship. Sean is prone to disappearing into his own little world and becomes easily confused, whilst Patricia is not quite as sprightly as she imagines herself to be, but there is a certain chemistry and we find ourselves warming to them both and wanting to know them better.

They seem to be getting on famously but then Patricia oversteps the mark. Misreading the signals she kisses Sean with passion. He is appalled. "You're old", he says, "you're a woman!", he then recovers himself to tell her that he has a love: Tom.

Tom doesn't visit any more. In a heartbreaking scene Sean describes how they have become incompatible. Sean has become old; they are no longer on the same wavelength. Patricia is angry on Sean's behalf but it is his acceptance which makes it so sad. Then, just when it seems that the mutual support that they are able to provide each other will bring their lives some meaning, Patricia is gone. We end as we began. Sean is alone again.

Halcyon Days is a touching comedy drama which never becomes over sentimental. The comedy is not at the expense of the characters but, rather, we get the sense that we are laughing with them. For example, when Sean tells Patricia that he goes for a rest after breakfast, she asks him what he is resting from. His reply, that he doesn't know, seems to amuse him as much as it does us. In all, I have no hesitation in recommending this script to any society looking for a play with two excellent roles for older performers.

HAPPY BIRTHDAY ME
Author: Simon Williams
Publisher: Samuel French
ISBN NO: 9780573120930
Cast: 2M 5F + Voice
Type: One Act

We are in an actor's retirement home (how many are there) where it is Margot Buchanon's seventieth birthday. As the play begins Margot's mobile telephone is ringing and it is answered by Freda, a fellow resident. Apparently it is Leo, Margot's ex, and Freda tells him that his former wife does not wish to speak to him.

It appears that Leo, himself an actor, is all over the papers after punching a journalist. Meanwhile, when she finds out what the other residents have planned for her birthday, Margot is fast running out of coins for the swear box. But that is just the start of her troubles. First Leo's current wife, Lady Buchanon, arrives then Leo himself turns up, on the run from the paparazzi. He couldn't have picked a worse time because Margot is currently receiving a visitor. A young actress who, it just so happens, is having an affair with Leo, the leaked story of this being what caused Leo to punch the journalist in the first place. It's all too much for the ageing lothario and even the presence of Supperman – a kissogram for Margot – can save him from having a heart attack.

The first part of this short play is peppered with brilliant one-liners but, after Leo's death, everyone starts being nice to each other and the comedy is lost. However, it does have a feel-good ending and some nice roles for older actresses.

HARRY RINGS, LORD OF THE POTTERS
Author: Alison Chaplin
Publisher: Arts on the Move
ISBN NO: 9781906153007
Cast: 20 Characters
Type: One Act

When I saw first saw the title of this piece I wondered if it might be a fantasy adventure set within the city of Stoke-on-Trent, but I suppose that would be stretching the imagination a bit too far! Instead we are at Hogwash school where the headmaster has a quest for Harry. Their enemy, "He Who cannot Be Named But Is Called Fred", has stolen the Goblet of Eternal Youth and anyone who drinks from this vessel will be granted ultimate power and everlasting life. Harry is instructed to locate the goblet and return it to its rightful place taking two of his friends to help him: the girl with the unpronounceable name and the gormless lad with the red hair.

Meanwhile, Gandalf the Purple has also sent a couple of his hoblins to locate the goblet and the two parallel journeys provide us with much entertainment until they all finally meet and decide to continue their journeys together. They eventually reach the cave of darkness and meet He Who Cannot – oh, let's just call him Fred – who appears to have the upper hand but Harry tricks him and is, naturally, the hero who saves the day.

The story has good pace and lots to amuse. The innate silliness of it all is quite endearing and I can imagine the play being enjoyed by audiences of all ages. I read a lot of plays for children that have 'something for the grown-ups' but quite often the 'something' goes over the heads of children whilst the main storyline does little to hold the interest of adults. The best children's plays are written in such a way that the adults and the children in the audience laugh at the same things and with Harry Rings, Lord of the Potters, Alison Chaplin has written a piece that does just that.

DAVID MUNCASTER

THE HAUNTING
Author: Hugh Janes – adapted from several stories by Charles Dickens.
Publisher: Nick Hern Books
ISBN NO: 9781848422155
Cast: 2M 1F
Type: Full Length

This is a play inspired by an event that happened to the author's uncle. Whilst visiting an old manor house to acquire some books for his antiquarian book shop, a woman appeared and observed him at his work. When she then disappeared without a sound Hugh Janes' uncle was convinced that he had seen a ghost. This event planted the idea and the author turned to Charles Dickens to help it bloom.

The play opens with David, a young book dealer, asleep in a wing chair in the study of a dusty old house. He is woken by Lord Gray who enters the room illuminating it with an oil lamp. David's weariness is due to the long journey from London which was delayed during the final leg when a woman threw herself in front of the carriage, scaring the horses. She begged David not to go to the house claiming that she knew the "secret of the tree"

Lord Gary assures David that there is nothing that should cause alarm and leaves him to his sleep so that business can commence in the morning. Odd, though, that he looks the door. Odder, still, is the voice of a woman who cannot be seen pleading to David to help her.

The following day there are more strange occurrences but Lord Gray will hear nothing of David's stories of books hurling themselves of shelves and he dismisses ghostly sounds as nothing more than ordinary domestic noises made to seem unnatural by an over active imagination. He even claims not to see a young woman in a tattered bridal gown sitting in the wing chair, but when he learns of David's connection with a woman from his own family's past he finds that he cannot ignore the evidence of his eyes and ears any longer.

There are things to admire in this script. David's impertinent humour provides light relief and is neatly explained once we learn of his connection with Lord Gray but, for a production to be successful, the audience would have to buy in to it (or enter into the spirit, if you will forgive the pun). This will require the special effects to be performed with great precision and the cast to react to them in a way that seems

62

genuine. Five Dickens stories make up this play and, at times, I felt I could see the joins, but nevertheless Hugh James has produced a script that could provide the basis of a spooky night at the theatre. It is up to the director and cast to make it work.

HERDING CATS
Author: Lucinda Coxon
Publisher: Nick Hern Books
ISBN NO: 9781848422407
Cast: 2M 1F
Type: Full Length

"I literally exploded" is Justine's opening line. She didn't, of course, otherwise she wouldn't be around to say it, but semantics don't worry Justine. She has enough to do just trying to cope with the twenty-first century. Life, for her, is like herding cats.

Meanwhile, her flatmate, Michael, has a job talking to strangers on the telephone. We listen to the disturbing conversation he has with one of his clients, known to us as Saddo, and wonder whether we are watching the creation of a fantasy or a recreation of actual events. Michael is agoraphobic and earns a living working for a telephone sex company. He claims to be detached from his clients.

Justine claims to hate her older boss but we are not sure who she is trying to kid. When she does give in and make an attempt at intimacy she is spurned and turns to Michael for comfort. The gift of a T shirt suggests to her that her flatmate has some feelings for her but the truth is that the photos he has just taken of her wearing it are to send to Saddo.

Herding Cats is a snapshot of lives that seem hectic but are, in fact, lonely and unfulfilling. It will not be to everybody's taste but it will strike a chord with many who see it.

THE HERESY OF LOVE
Author: Helen Edmundson
Publisher: Nick Hern Books
ISBN NO: 97818484222391
Cast: 7M 8F
Type: Full Length

Sor Juana Inés de la Cruz was a poet, nun and major literary figure in seventeenth century Mexico. Her success as a writer of plays for the court led to problems with the church and persecution from a zealous archbishop in whose palace the play begins.

As a new incumbent of the role the archbishop has summoned senior members of his church to answer questions. In particular he wants to know why Bishop Santa Cruz had, earlier that evening, attended the performance of a play at court. He is told that this is not unusual in Mexico City, but the archbishop intends to change all that.

Sister Juana has her supporters, each with their own motives, but there are also those who have previously celebrated her work who now take the side of the archbishop. As the story builds the atmosphere becomes highly charged. Sister Juana is not the only resident of the convent to receive visits from lustful church seniors but greatest tension comes when the viceroy of Mexico requests that Sister Juana writes a play to celebrate his forthcoming parenthood: a request that puts church and state on a collision course.

The pace quickens as everything comes to a head. The church orders burning of books - secular plays and poems are to be replaced in the book stores by religious texts. The viceroy decides that he is to leave Mexico and, with the city in a state of upheaval, Bishop Santa Cruz encourages Sister Juana to write an essay about the archbishop. It is supposed to be for his eyes only but he publishes it. This leads to Sister Juana being forced to sign a confession which she does so in blood. Meanwhile, sickness has overtaken the convent and soon, with a storm of a biblical nature raging outside, Sister Juana is dead.

Throughout the entire script the dialogue is captivating. Sister Juana speaks with a modest wisdom that casts a spell on those who hear her and Helen Edmundson's play about her holds the attention from start to finish.

HOME DEATH
Author: Nell Dunn
Publisher: Nick Hern Books
ISBN NO: 9781848421950
Cast: 5M 6F
Type: Full Length

Research predicts that by 2013, 90% of us will die in a hospital ward, whilst the majority of us would wish to end our lives in our own homes.

In Home Death Null Dunn explores how people cope with the death of their loved ones in the kind of circumstances for which few of us feel prepared. In keeping with her most famous works, she uses stories from real life, including her own, to cast a critical eye over palatial care in the UK and question society's responsibility for looking after their own.

The characters take it in turn to tell us their stories that carry a common theme of helplessness. The author reserves the strongest sense of regret for her own tale. "I was shocked at some of the things I said", she explains, "I can't wash your feet today, I haven't time", and "no you can't have a stairlift because it would spoil the carpet".

But the overwhelming theme is the different levels of care that people experience – or perhaps it is just their own perception of that care. However, there can be no excuse for the doctor who is called out on a Sunday morning, argues with the nurse, consults his notebook, writes a prescription and leaves without once speaking, or even looking at, the patient. "Thank you for coming" says Nell. His response is that she shouldn't worry – he gets paid very well for call outs.

It is impossible to read this play without becoming emotionally involved. It is nearly forty years since my own mother died, at home as it happens, but I immediately identified with the anguish felt by the characters in this thought provoking and deeply moving play.

THE HOUND OF THE BASKERVILLES
Author: Steven Canny and John Nicholson from the story by Sir Arthur Conan Doyle
Publisher: Nick Hern Books
ISBN NO: 9781848422421
Cast: 3M
Type: Full Length

Patrick Barlow's adaptation of John Buchan's The 39 Steps has been a global success and here we see another piece of classic literature getting the spoof treatment. However, it would be unfair to accuse Canny and Nicholson of bandwagon jumping. Their version of The Hound of the Baskervilles was first performed at the West Yorkshire Playhouse in 2007 two years after The 39 Steps received its first performance at the same venue but, although The 39 Steps was by this time playing in New York, it had not yet become a worldwide hit.

Nevertheless, it is hard not to draw comparisons. The formula is the same: a small cast play multiple characters in a very fast paced comedy that is based on a story that will already be familiar to a large number of the audience. But, whereas The 39 Steps is Pythonesque in its humour, stiff upper-lippedness being the key to much of the comedy, The Hound of the Baskervilles is more reminiscent of the gloriously surreal TV show The Mighty Boosh.

In the original production the actor who played, amongst others, Sherlock Holmes was Spanish, and the script was written to accommodate this. The authors have included some alternative lines for him, but personally I prefer the Spanish version.

As the house lights dim the play stops before it has even started. Actor 3 is prostrate on the stage, playing the part of the deceased Sir Charles Baskerville, when Actor 2 rushes on halting the performance because they have neglected to make an important safety announcement. Anyone who had come to the theatre expecting a straight play is put right within seconds and even given the opportunity to leave. "Don't worry: no one will look at you." assures Actor 2 before introducing the actor who will be Sherlock Holmes who greets us with a polite "Buenas Nochas".

This is a silly beginning to a very silly play, but I'm not complaining. Silly is good. Silly is very good. Whilst they have a lot of fun spoofing the original story, I think my favourite moment comes immediately after the interval when the actors read out a tweet that a member of the audience has supposedly sent to Twitter. They are so incensed by the comment that they decide that they will perform act one again, which they do at a breakneck speed in a couple of minutes. Then it is on with the story and straight back to the moor and the unravelling of the mystery that surrounds the ancient curse of the Hound of the Baskervilles. Watson complains about the complexity of it all but as he muses on "Rare moths, Brazilian identities, wives pretending to be sisters. We're lost in an incestuous, South America, menagerie of intolerable dead ends." he need not despair. The answers lie in the portraits on the wall of the snooker room and before very long the perpetrator of the heinous crimes on the moor is, quite literally, sunk.

When I directed The 39 Steps it was the highlight of everything that I have done so far in amateur theatre. I'd love to repeat that success but always imagined that I would steer clear of anything that was similar. However, having read this script I am tempted. Very tempted!

THE HOUSE KEEPER
Author: Morna Regan
Publisher: Nick Hern Books
ISBN NO: 9781848422728
Cast: 1M 2F
Type: Full Length

I'm puzzling over why "house keeper" is two words in the title. Does this suggest that it is meant to mean something different from "housekeeper"? As the play begins we find Mary toiling with an old fashioned carpet sweeper but having little effect on a musty old Persian rug that dominates the floor space. It would appear that Mary is, indeed, the housekeeper in this run down Manhattan mansion except that it is the middle of the night and when Beth, the owner of the house, enters the room she is brandishing a hammer, ready to deal with an intruder.

We assume that there must be some sort of misunderstanding but we learn that Mary really is an intruder. She has broken into the house and is cleaning the rug in order to lay down some bed rolls for herself and her children, who are currently asleep in the car. Mary has lost her own home. She has seen Beth around for many years and resents her; resents the fact that she has this big house and plenty of money without ever having to lift a finger whilst Mary has worked all her life but she has lost her job in the recession, the bank has taken away her house and, now, social services are after her children.

"This is lunacy", says Beth. She might be referring to her own circumstances. Mary assumes her to be a widow but then Hal, Beth's husband, enters. For the last fifteen years he has been suffering from a disease that affects his motor functions and Beth has been his nurse. Refusing help from outside agencies Hal has insisted that Beth performs her "wifely duties" which consist of providing him with constant care in spite of the tirade of abuse that he constantly throws at her.

Then Beth has an idea. If Mary wants her house she can have it: and everything in it, including Hal. So this is the explanation of the two words of the title. One of the women will keep the house, whilst the other one loses it. As Mary battles with her conscience Beth and Hal, as they have for the last decade and a half, battle with each other.

There is a vein of dark humour running through this play that elevates it from being quite a mundane thriller but I feel that the author has, on occasion, gone out of her way to shock which is all rather unnecessary. I would have preferred it if she had spent her energy developing the characters in which case I might have actually cared what happened to them. As it is I am left unmoved.

HUNDREDS AND THOUSANDS
Author: Lou Ramsden
Publisher: Nick Hern Books
ISBN NO: 9781848422124
Cast: 2M 2F
Type: Full Length

An isolated farmhouse: a little run down; dated and cluttered; clocks that tick a fusty tick. Lorna, forty-three, is moving in. Helping her is her brother, Jonathan, who does not hide his unease about the situation. Their father has died and the family home has been sold leaving Lorna without a place to live. So, she is moving in with her boyfriend even though she has only known him for six months and has never been to the farmhouse before. Jonathan looks around the place. Yes, there is clutter but a lot of it is expensive clutter: stuff he wouldn't mind having in his antique shop. But there is something not-quite-right and, beneath the sibling banter, the tension is building nicely.

This is broken by the chimes of an ice-cream van which herald the arrival of Allan, Lorna's boyfriend. The author brings out the humour here well. Allan tells Lorna that he would have helped her move in but, as his means of transport is incapable of exceeding ten miles per hour, it isn't really practical. He teases Jonathan until he leaves and the happy couple get down to some smooching on the sofa when we hear the tinkling of a bell. "It's just Tiggy looking for a fuss." explains Allan. Lorna is keen to meet the cat, so long as she doesn't scratch, and calls her. But Tiggy isn't a cat. She is a thirty-two year old woman dressed in filthy home-made clothes with her hands tied and a dog's collar round her neck.

Naturally, Lorna's first thought is to flee, even though she is twenty miles from anywhere, but Allan forces her to listen to his explanation. Tiggy was left at the farmhouse when she was a child – abandoned like a cat. Allan's mother took her in and raised her, but kept her a secret. Allan describes Tiggy as 'simple-minded' and says they were worried the authorities would take her away. So she lives in the cellar and earns her keep by cleaning and tidying, frightened to leave the house in case she is caught by 'Hatters' – the monsters that she has been told live in the woods surrounding the farmhouse.

Lorna decides to stay, though her acceptance of the situation seems a little far-fetched. Perhaps she is intrigued; perhaps she thinks she can help. Or perhaps she is just desperate. The clock is ticking and Allan could be her last chance to ever have children. As the weeks pass, Lorna descends into a kind of madness, her cruelty toward Tiggy making Allan's behaviour seem almost normal.

Hundreds and Thousands has periods of dark humour reminiscent of Steve Pemberton's and Reece Shearsmith's TV programme, Psychoville, but I fear that audiences may find it difficult to suspend disbelief long enough to enjoy this play.

I AM SHAKESPEARE
Author: Mark Rylance
Publisher: Nick Hern Books
ISBN NO: 9781848422698
Cast: 6M 1F
Type: Full Length

The authorship of Shakespeare's plays is something that has puzzled scholars for years. How could the son of an illiterate tradesman have written the greatest dramatic works the world has ever seen? Fortunately, I'm no scholar and it isn't a question that has troubled me much. Shakespeare's father was the richest man in Stratford- upon-Avon and could certainly have afforded to give his son a good education. Furthermore, I do not believe it is necessary to be a member of the aristocracy in order to write about them. Haven't many of the world's greatest artists come from humble beginnings?

Nevertheless it is a debate that has sold a lot of books and now celebrated Shakespearian actor, Mark Rylance, has used it as the subject of his first play.

The play is set in Frank's Garage. Frank is a schoolteacher and obsessive researcher of the authorship question. From his garage he presents a weekly webcast Who's There?; a live internet chat show that "dares to ask the question who really wrote the works of William Shakespeare?" Just as the show is about to begin, Barry, Frank's neighbour calls in. Barry is, or rather was, a pop star who had one hit twenty years ago and now makes up jingles and investigates crop circles (sounds like Reg Presley of The Troggs to me). The show survives the disturbance caused by Barry's search for guttering but when he sneaks out and telephones the show, pretending to be Derek Jacobi, (with a Scottish accent) it all starts to be a bit too much for Frank.

But things are about to get worse. The next visitor is someone who could claim to be a bit of an authority on the works of William Shakespeare: William Shakespeare himself. Somehow, through the magic of the internet, the bard has appeared in Frank's garage and presents a very compelling argument. Frank is convinced. Of course Shakespeare wrote the plays himself. Now that Frank can see this, no one will convince him otherwise. This is until Francis Bacon turns up.

Bacon adopts a curious stance: rather than try to convince Frank that it was he that wrote the plays, he argues that Shakespeare did not. However the next guest, Edward De Vere, is much more forthright in his claims; so forthright, in fact, that someone calls the police. Whilst the police sergeant draws parallels between the authorship question and the identity of Jack the Ripper the arrival of yet another guest presents yet another argument. Mary Sidney claims that the bard was not one person – that the plays were actually written by a pool of writers but, and this is the point, does it matter? Surely it is the plays that are important, not the identity of who wrote them.

As if to emphasise this point the play concludes with the police sergeant returning in order to arrest Shakespeare and demands to know which one is he. Having just seen a clip from the film I Spartacus the cast and if they are game, the audience, are all inspired to declare "I am Shakespeare!"

There is a lot about this script that annoys me. It is littered with author's notes which even Mark Rylance admits he cannot understand. He also admits that it is too long and suggests lines that might be cut. Why present a play for publication that you believe to be imperfect? If it weren't't for who the author was any publisher would have rejected it; which would be a tragedy as this is a very funny play indeed: a delight from start to finish which should have an audience roaring with laughter and joyfully participating in the conclusion. A remarkable first play that deserves to earn Mark Rylance a reputation as a writer to match the one he has an actor.

I'LL EAT YOU LAST
Author: John Logan
Publisher: Oberon Modern Plays
ISBN NO: 9781849434140
Cast: 1F
Type: Monologue

The subtitle of this play is A Chat With Sue Mengers: Sue being a Hollywood agent with a lot of secrets to tell. The play was first performed in New York in 2013 with Bette Midler in the role.

We are in Sue Menger's tastefully decorated Beverly Hills home. As she speaks she is smoking constantly. In the 1970s Sue represented just about every major star in Hollywood but it is now 1981 and the glory days are over.

She is waiting for a call from Barbra Streisand who sacked her today. Rather, the lawyers sacked her and she has been promised a call from Barbra herself tonight. She is talking to an unseen interviewer but she also acknowledges the audience. The fourth wall has already been broken with glances and frowns when, wanting something slightly out of reach on her coffee table, she selects a member of the audience to come up onto the stage to fetch it for her. From this point forward this person is referred to in the script as Unlucky Audience Member and is called upon several times.

Sue tells us her life story. Her family fled the Nazis to come to America and she became what she describes as "a fat little Jewess who spoke no English." But she had a determination that was to prove useful in later life and was soon making friends. She started out wanting to be an actress but was hindered by a lack of talent - "not that it matters these days" - so instead got a job as a receptionist at a talent agency. One night she saw Barbara (still with three As back then) perform in a night club and recognised the potential. Streisand became her first client and opened the door for many more.

We are led through an A list of celebrities, that Sue has represented over the years, and she relishes in dishing the dirt to the maximum. Because these are real people, the author has had to take care with what Sue tells us, all of it being verifiable facts, but the way it is presented makes it feel as though we are being trusted with secrets. Eventually Sue misjudges something and her reputation is in ruins. She loses clients by the dozen; a fact that she acknowledges when she tells us of her relish for the film The Poseidon Adventure where she sees so many of her former clients get drowned. We're not sure if she ever does get the phone call from Barbra but one thing we know for certain is that Sue Mengers will survive, whatever happens.

I don't know if this play was written specifically for Bette Midler but it is very easy to imagine her in the role. For that reason it might be difficult for any other actress to carry it off, but it is an entertaining romp which I am sure an audience would enjoy; with the possible exception of Unlucky Audience Member.

IGNORANCE/JAHILIYYAH
Author: Steve Waters
Publisher: Nick Hern Books
ISBN NO: 9781848422957
Cast: 3M 2F
Type: Full Length

Sayyid Qutb was born in Egypt in 1906. The son of a politically active landowner Qutb was critical of the way religion had such influence on politics and how schools neglected academic study in favour of religion in his country. In 1949 he went to study in America and this was to have a major influence on his thinking. He was shocked by the lack of faith, the materialism and the level of promiscuity. He returned to Egypt and joined the Muslim Brotherhood and became later Head of Propaganda. In 1966 he was executed for his part in the assassination of the Egyptian president Gamel Abdel Nasser.

In Steve Water's play Philip Mitchell, a professor at a London university, is writing a book about Qutb. He enters his office with the intention of eating lunch but is surprised to find a student waiting for him. This is Layla, a young student from Egypt who is in London to study under Professor Mitchell. She is in his office because she wants to be under his supervision instead of the professor to whom she is currently assigned, Dr Nassir Al-Malaki, who describes Mitchell as "an apologiser for terror". Layla and Professor Mitchell are wary of each other, their motives are unclear, but both seem to want something that they believe the other can provide.

The action then moves from present day London to Greesley, Colorado in 1949 where Qutb began his American studies. In the college refectory

Wayne and Myrna are eating lunch when Qutb joins them and asks to be passed the condiments. The epitome of politeness Wayne tells Qutb that he has made a mistake: international students are required to sit together in the atrium.

The opening scenes of the play are promising. The relationships between Professor Mitchell and Layla in London and Myrna and Qutb in Colorado begin to develop, influenced by an odd mixture of goodwill, mistrust and, as the title of the play suggests, ignorance. However, as the play continued, I found the motivation behind Professor Mitchell and Layla's posturing quite difficult to fathom and something of a distraction from the more interesting narrative of Qutb's radicalisation in America.

The thing that I love about theatre is that nothing is taboo and Steve Waters is obviously not afraid to write about sensitive subjects. However, I think that Ignorance/Jahiliyyah perhaps tries too hard to be abstruse and, as a result, is quite hard work.

INTERVALS
Author: Eleanor Fossey
Publisher: J Garnett Miller
ISBN NO: 9780853436836
Cast: Min 1M 2F + 1 extra
Type: One Act

Intervals comprises three sketches that can be performed on their own or all together. Set during performances of Goldilocks and the Three Bears, the first sketch features Bernice and Deirdre who, to their dismay, are playing Mummy and Daddy Bear. This is the eleventh performance and Bernice has been driven to drink. Sitting alone in her dressing room she knocks back the vodka before being joined by Deirdre who shares both the dressing room and the vodka.

As they vent their frustrations at being cast in such lowly positions, they work their way through cast and crew with hardly a kind word for anyone. Amongst the bitterness there are some nice teddy jokes. Bernice sums up the situation nicely with her line, "Please don't stroke the bears, 'cos they bite."

The second sketch finds us in the dressing room of Sophie. Although as Principle Boy she has the luxury of a room that she shares with just one other, Goldilocks, she is currently on her own and she allows her friend from the chorus, Gina, to come in and escape from the irritating Baby Bear who is showing off with her iPod and mobile. It is Sophie, however, who is in real trouble. She has heard that the men at the theatre are planning to amuse themselves with a screening of a mucky video after the show tonight, this particular one being one of a series starring none other than Sophie herself. Explaining to Gina that she made the films when she was just starting out in the business and desperate for money, she is mortified that her past has caught up with her and flees from the theatre having persuaded Gina to squeeze into her costume and go on in her place.

This sketch seemed a little flat after the shenanigans of the first one. The jokes seemed a bit forced and I had difficulty believing that Sophie would throw everything away over something that she must have known would come to light if she ever became famous.

On to the last sketch which finds us in the company of Betty and Doris who are manning the sweet counter during the interval of the final performance of this pantomime. The gossiping pair mull over rumours about Sophie's departure and, between serving customers, give us their opinions about everyone involved in the production.

Again, the jokes are a bit awkward, as though they have been inserted to bring a few laughs but without really fitting in with the dialogue. However, put it all together and you have an entertaining, if not particularly demanding, glimpse behind the scenes of regional theatre at panto time.

INVISIBLE
Author: Tena Štivičić
Publisher: Nick Hern Books
ISBN NO: 97818484223600
Cast: 4M 3F with doubling
Type: Full Length

Invisible is a play that explores issues of migration. The characters are seeking their place in the world; both physically and spiritually. For Felix, Eastern Europe is an emerging market: a place where his wind turbines can generate electricity in line with European Union directives about renewable energy.

This 'emerging market' is home to Lara, but it is a home that cannot sustain her. She travels to Britain convinced that her talents in designing and making clothes will lead to great things. Anton has his own reasons for leaving his village and, arriving in the UK, finds it hard to distinguish between truth, hearsay and fairy-tales.

Tena Štivičić makes good use of irony as Felix views Serbia as a place of freedom; somewhere that regulations do not get in the way of profit. But, of course, for many of the local population, freedom means fleeing to the west.

If all this sounds a bit grim, I should say that there is plenty of well executed humour in the script. Felix picks up Lara in a nightclub unaware that she is actually employed in his own home as a housekeeper. When he opens the door to her the next morning the farcical situation also gives us an opportunity to learn a bit more about Felix.

Theatre commonly reflects contemporary issues and there are lots of plays being produced about migration. What makes Invisible a bit different is that it has the feel of a novel. It is fitting that Felix makes a reference to A Brief History of Tractors in Ukrainian because, like Marina Lewycka's celebrated book, Tena Štivičić's script has equal measures of humour, poignancy and hope.

JUDGEMENT DAY
Author: Mike Poulton
Publisher: Nick Hern Books
ISBN NO: 9781848422414
Cast: 4M 3F
Type: Full Length

When We Dead Awaken was Henrik Ibsen's last play, first performed in 1899 but rarely performed today. Mike Poulton, the "adaptor of the moment" according to The Observer, has now added this play to his list of classics transformed for a modern audience.

The original play was autobiographical. Ibsen cast himself as an elderly artist talking to other artists about the difficulties brought about by that most wonderful of human emotions, love, on his artistic objectivity. In Judgement Day Ibsen, as Arnold Rubek, a rich and successful sculpture, is holidaying at a health spa with his young wife Maia. Maia is bored: bored with the holiday and bored with her husband. In their four years of marriage the couple have learnt to loathe each other.

During the night Rubek believes that he sees a ghost in the wood: a white figure being followed by a black figure. But it is no ghost. It is Irena De Satoff and her companion, who happens to be a nun, who are taking the night air. Later Irena comes to the terrace where Rubek and Maia are having breakfast and, after Maia has gone off with Ultheim, a hunter, to see his dogs, we learn that Rubek and Irena know each other. Many years ago she was his muse. She was the inspiration for every sculpture he has ever done; it was her body that he modelled from the stone. She gave birth to his art, yet he abandoned her.

Rubek now realises that, for all her youth and beauty, Maia cannot offer him something that Irena can: an understanding of his art. Maia accepts this, suggesting that they all live together at their villa not realising that Irena harbours a murderous hatred for Rubek. In the end though, it is nature, not revenge, that takes their lives.

Poulton has done well to turn Ibsen's almost impenetrable script into a coherent piece of theatre but, though it is interesting to get glimpse into the mind of the genius, I do not believe that this play is the sort to have a very wide appeal.

JUMPERS FOR GOALPOSTS
Author: Tom Wells
Publisher: Nick Hern Books
ISBN NO: 9781848423268
Cast: 4M 1F plus one voice
Type: Full Length

The play begins with a voice from the radio reading football results. In the original production this voice was provided by James Alexander Gordon who, for as long as I can remember, has communicated the results on the BBC every Saturday. However, I have never heard him read out a scoreline such as Lesbian Rovers 5, Barely Athletic 0!

Viv is the captain of the losing team above that has been so roundly thrashed and she is not happy. She seems to be the only one taking it seriously: Luke just wants to get home to his Dad's Yorkshire Puddings; Joe's in a strop because Viv has had a go at him about his fitness; Danny fancies Luke but has a secret reason why he cannot ask him out, and Geoff, a busker, dreams of playing the stage at Hull Pride and becoming a gay icon.

The following week the team has been beaten 7 - 0 by Man City (in this case Man is just Man; it isn't short for Manchester) and Viv has decided that the team needs coaching. She has a book about coaching junior football teams: Geoff thinks that's a bit harsh but Viv tells him that the shop didn't have a book for coaching toddlers. She just wants them to have a go. Losing is bad enough but losing when you haven't really been trying is much worse. She seems to have struck a chord: the following week they win, beating Tranny United 4-1.

What's changed? For one thing Geoff has stopped sleeping with the opposition, though that was no great hardship. The last time, in the middle of all the action the music playing in the background changed to Enya. It isn't easy being passionate to a soundtrack of Orinoco Flow!

Things are going well: the team is progressing up the Hull Gay and Lesbian Five-a-Side Football League and Danny and Luke are finally getting it together. But there is also tension. Danny's secret is becoming the elephant in the room and we, the audience, have started to love the characters and want everything to be all right. Finally, Danny tells Luke; he has HIV. "Why didn't you tell me?", demands Luke. "Quite a big thing to tell someone.", explains Danny. "Quite a big thing not to tell someone.", counters Luke.

Luke panics: leaves and doesn't turn up the following week. But we eventually get reconciliation and even though the end is cheesy, perhaps deliberately so, we are happy that things could be OK.

Tom Wells has already demonstrated his talent with plays like The Kitchen Sink and Me, As A Penguin, but with Jumpers for Goalposts he has written a play that is warm, funny and accessible. This is a very enjoyable, poignant but thoroughly entertaining play.

JUST THE TICKET
Author: Peter Quilter
Publisher: Samuel French
ISBN NO: 9780573112270
Cast: 1F
Type: Full Length

There is one character in this play, Susan, but the author has suggested that, should the director desire it, the role could be shared between several actresses thereby putting a different spin on the same character. Like James Bond. Well, perhaps not much like James Bond.

As a one woman play, Just The Ticket is bound to draw comparisons with Shirley Valentine but, whereas Shirley is having a mid-life crisis, Susan is having a whole-life crisis. She has decided to celebrate her sixtieth birthday by reliving a holiday she had with a group of friends when she was twenty. The destination, Australia, is the same, but this time she is alone.

We begin at the airport where Susan chats nervously to anyone who will listen. She also chats nervously to people who don't want to listen; she just chats regardless. Whilst she is the only character on the stage her gestures make it easy for us to imagine the people with whom she comes into contact, and to imagine their embarrassment as Susan, yet again, says the wrong thing at the wrong time.

Having arrived in Australia she heads for the same hotel where she finds the same barman, Bill, still serving at the bar. She orders four cocktails to represent the friends on that first visit, and becomes amusingly tipsy as she describes how each of them eventually moved on, leaving her behind.

The holiday seems like a bad idea, serving as a reminder of how lonely Susan has become, but perhaps Bill might bring a bit of joy to Susan's life? She goes out and buys a new dress, and shoes that make walking impossible, but she insists that she is not smitten. Then comes the saddest moment in the play when she kicks off the shoes and begins to dance. The sadness in her eyes turns to joy as she imagines being swept around the room by the man of her dreams but poignancy follows when the music stops and Susan reflects that if a man is ever going to want her then she will have to change; to stop being herself.

I have no doubt that throughout the course of the play any audience will have grown to love Susan; so much so that they will being praying for some morsel of hope for a better future. Her self- depreciating humour, her inappropriate comments, even her tendency to be a tiny bit bitchy about people who have let her down have all combined to endear this eccentric old lady to us and, thank goodness, the play ends with a glimmer of hope.

Good luck, Susan. I hope it works out for you.

KES
Author: Robert Alan Evans, adapted for the stage from A Kestrel for a Knave by Barry Hines
Publisher: Samuel French
ISBN NO: 9780573150234
Cast: 2M
Type: Full Length

One of the challenges of adapting a well known story is living up to expectations of capturing what that story means to the people who are familiar with the original. I suspect, that like most people, I am more familiar with the film than the book and, to me, the story was about a boy finding his identity. My memories are made up of images: the bullying on the football field; the escape from the shower; the awkward interview with the career advisor and, of course, the spectacular sight of the kestrel hawk soaring through the sky and coming back to Billy, displaying a trust that the boy, himself, found in few humans.

This play is for two actors: a boy plays Billy whilst another actor, the man, plays all the other roles. We see the latter as Billy's brother, Jud, sharing his bed then stealing his bicycle to go to his job down the pit making Billy late for his paper round. The actor then becomes Mr Porter, the newsagent, complaining about boys who, like Billy, live on "the estate", but it is when the actor becomes Billy's mum that we get the first sign of Billy's tragic life. His mother asking him for a fag, or some money to buy some, still seems shocking – illustrative of how he is being denied his childhood by the one person who is supposed to care for him the most.

Later, as the career advisor is apparently doing his best to help Billy make a decision on his future, the boy's mind is elsewhere: specifically, the bet that he neglected to put on for his brother and what Jud might do to punish him should the horse win.

Robert Alan Evans captures the spirit of the story very well and without resorting to gimmickry. As the actor playing multiple roles becomes a new character he announces who he is so that they can get straight on with the narrative, and the training of the hawk is simply left to our imagination. Billy is a constant bundle of energy and lives for the moment whilst the man has a sadness about him that suggests he knows the tragedy that is to come but, when we do reach the emotional climax, it is the man that persuades Billy that there is always hope, no matter what life throws at you.

THE KITCHEN SINK
Author: Tom Wells
Publisher: Nick Hern Books
ISBN NO: 9781848422223
Cast: 3M 2F
Type: Full Length

"What do you think about the nipples? Mum?" Now there's an opening line! This is Billy, who is hoping that his portrait of Dolly Parton is going to earn him a place at Art College. "Mum" is Kath, busy chopping vegetables for the evening meal and not really having much time for all this but she is a good mum tries to be supportive.

Life is a bit of a struggle for this family at the moment. On top of Billy's concerns about getting into college, his sister, Sophie, can see her dreams of becoming a ju-jitsu teacher disappearing down the plug hole. Speaking of which; what is that smell coming from the sink? And why is there a bit of a milk float on the kitchen table?

Enter Martin: husband, father and failing milkman. It would appear that he has had more customers cancel their milk that Kath has cooked hot dinners – and for the last 25 years she has been a school dinner lady.

When the play begins it is spring and, as the seasons come and go, life stumbles on. Sophie tries to teach her brother some self defence moves with the help of her sort-of boyfriend, Pete. Meanwhile, any chance she had of becoming a ju-jitsu teacher vanished when she decked the examiner, and she is now helping her dad on the milk round. Billy is having second thoughts about going to college but he goes after his mum asks him what is there for him in Withensea? Things don't work out for him but he always has his family to fall back on.

That is what the play is about really: people supporting each other, even though that support is not always welcomed. So much in modern life is unreliable: not just milk floats and sinks but even our dreams and what we think we want for ourselves. But, as Martin wryly comments, there is more to life than milk. So what did Kath think of Dolly Parton's nipples? Perfect. Spot on. Just like Dolly Parton. On a cold day.

LABURNUM GROVE

Author: J B Priestley
Publisher: Oberon Modern Plays
ISBN NO: 9781849434928
Cast: 6M 3F
Type: Full Length

George Radfern is a decent and respectable citizen. He has worked hard all his life and this has meant that he has been able to buy a nice house in one of North London's newer suburbs where he spends his Sunday evenings pottering about in his greenhouse before sitting down for a pleasant cold supper with his wife, Dorothy.

However, it is not all peace and harmony. Staying with them is his wife's sister, Lucy, and her husband, Bernard. Unlike George, Bernard has not worked hard all his life: he is more of a chancer and his latest scheme is to invest in a business that he is sure will succeed. In order to take advantage of this opportunity he needs to borrow £450, a not inconsiderable sum in 1933. "We'll discuss it after supper", says George.

George also has a daughter, Elsie, who has a young man, Harold. They are planning to get engaged but, first, Harold wants to "get himself set up". He knows of a business for sale and wants to borrow the money in order to buy it. He too is told by George that it will be discussed after supper.

With Dorothy not yet home, they sit down to eat and during the meal both Bernard and Harold are falling over themselves to stress their decency. Both claim to have had the opportunity to receive money that is "tainted" but neither of them would touch it: they have principles and would never associate themselves with anything that involved dishonesty.

They have, in fact, set themselves up very nicely for George to drop his bombshell. He tells them that his wholesale paper supply business went to the wall years ago. Since that time he has made a very nice living forging banknotes!

The next day George is much amused by the effect his story had on his guests. He leaves on a business trip with a spring in his step and a glint in his eye. Could he have made the whole thing up? As we ponder this an inspector calls. No, not that one, but the effect on Lucy and Bernard is

81

similar to that of Inspector Goole on the Birlings in J B Priestley's most celebrated play. They are horrified and make plans to flee after repeating the story George told them to Dorothy. Her response is to pick up a book from the table and tell her sister that if she wants to know how the story ends she should read it herself. Everything George told them is taken straight out of its pages.

So what is the truth? Is George a master criminal or a master leg-puller? The final scene sees a game of cat and mouse as George and the inspector attempt to outwit each other until the truth is finally revealed. Then, in a style typical of the author, the final curtain falls with us sure that the story is not yet over.

It is good that renewed interest in J B Priestley has led to some of his lesser known works being re-published. I wouldn't describe this as a lost masterpiece but it is a cracking good yarn that will keep the audience guessing right up to the end.

THE LADYKILLERS
Author: Graham Lineham from the screenplay by William Rose
Publisher: Samuel French
ISBN NO: 9780573112256
Cast: 6M 3F
Type: Full Length

Some of the pleasures of my childhood were experienced on wet Sunday afternoons watching Ealing comedies on the television: Whiskey Galore, The Lavender Hill Mob, Passport to Pimlico and, of course, The Ladykillers with the wonderful Katie Johnson as dotty old Mrs Wilberforce and Alec Guinness as Professor Marcus. When I read that there had been a stage adaptation of this classic I was in two minds. The comedy is certainly timeless but could the writer capture the magic of the silver screen. Graham Lineham certainly has pedigree. As the creator of TV programmes such as Father Ted and Black Books he has proven that he knows how to make people laugh, but how would he fare taking something that is already very funny and trying to make it work on a stage?

We begin at Mrs Wilberforce's slightly subsided Kings Cross home. It is 1956 and Mrs W is concerned that her grocer might be a Nazi. He has a funny accent (It turns out that he is from Burnley.) and during the war she wrote some rather stiff letters to Mr Hitler. Perhaps she is being targeted. Why else would he be asking her where she lives? The patient Constable Macdonald sips his tea and points out that it is probably because Mrs W has just put a card in the grocer's window advertising rooms to let. Oh yes. Silly Mrs W.

Before we know it, the doorbell rings and there stands Professor Marcus. "The room is perfect", he tells Mrs W. He doesn't mind the noise of the trains rattling by or the fact that nothing is quite straight. He doesn't even mind General Gordon, Mrs W's almost bald parrot, thankfully unseen by the audience. Everything will be fine so long as Mrs W doesn't object to him asking a few friends round. He is a member of a small musical group and they need somewhere to rehearse.

If you are not familiar with the story I should explain that this musical group is in fact the most unlikely and incompetent gang of criminals you are ever likely to come across and that they are planning a robbery of a security van as it delivers to nearby Kings Cross Station. Remarkably, they manage to pull it off, even involving Mrs W in transporting the loot back to the house.

But this is where it all starts to go wrong. In an incident of clumsiness one of the gang's cases falls open and Mrs W sees the money. In another incident of clumsiness one of the gang's mouths falls open and Mrs W hears that the money is from the robbery. What are they to do? At that moment some of Mrs W's friends appear expecting to be entertained by the Professor's musical group and the gang decide they have to keep up appearances. The interval will as a merciful relief from the miserable cacophony of scratching which the band call music.

Act two and the gang are faced with the problem of what to do with Mrs W. Bump her off seems to be the obvious answer and bumping off commences almost immediately. But Mrs W is not a victim.

This adaptation is a glorious success. I'm sure that anyone with fond memories of the film will enjoy it just as much as anyone to whom it is all new. It would be a challenge: the script calls for a revolving set and, whilst I don't believe that this is strictly necessary, I do think the various settings need to look authentic for the play to work. The comedy is delightful, and although most of it follows the screenplay there is also a fair amount of invention from Graham Lineham. Done well, this is a show that would live long in the memories of anyone lucky enough to see it.

LAGAN
Author: Stacey Greig
Publisher: Nick Hern Books
ISBN NO: 9781848422315
Cast: 5M 5F Doubling Possible
Type: Full Length

The Lagan is the river that runs through Belfast, one constant in a city that has seen a lot of change. Stacey Greig's play presents us with a kaleidoscope of stories from ten characters that can be played by a minimum of four actors.

So how much has Belfast changed since 'the troubles'? They say that if you want to know what's happening you should ask a taxi driver and here we have the bigoted and opinionated Taximan to tell us about how his city has gone from 'Beirut to EasyJet Top City Pick' in the space of ten years. With vegetarian restaurants and a much more cosmopolitan population, Taximan does not approve of everything that has happened but life goes on.

The other characters weave their way into the story. There is Ian who fled to England to escape his mother but is back to find his teenage sister terminating her pregnancy; Joan who has lost one son but has another who discovers love with Fiona; and then there are Taximan's children. All have one thing in common: "Belfast", they say, is the "blood and bone" of them.

The play has an interesting structure and the connections between the characters keep one interested. There is no doubting Stacey Greig's ability as a writer but I wonder if she sometimes delves too deeply into the hearts and minds of her characters at the expense of substance.

THE LAST GROUP
Author: Alison Gilmour
Publisher: J Garnett Miller
ISBN NO: 9780853436850
Cast: 2M 4F
Type: One Act

We are in a room set up for an art lesson. As the characters arrive the atmosphere is light and friendly and the audience would be forgiven for imagining that they are about to see a gentle, middle-class comedy of manners. But the arrival of newcomer, Stella, reveals that this is an Art Therapy group and the classroom is located within a largely disused psychiatric hospital. The group meets every Tuesday, when they discuss the week gone by, encouraged by their therapist, Theresa. This week, however, Theresa is nowhere to be found, despite her car being in the car park.

The group decide to press on without her and we learn their back stories. Sheila has depression but she has had a good week which included meeting one of the others, Maria, for a coffee. John also suffers from depression and his week has been like any other during which he has been henpecked by his wife who calls him 'an idiot' and 'a waste of space'. Malcolm doesn't want to start without Theresa there but does reveal that he is writing a book, which he proudly describes as being about a virus that spreads around the earth changing the basic DNA of everything it encounters. "Like in Spiderman", comments Stella.

Maria has intrusive thoughts about harming children and, though she would never carry out what she imagines, it makes going out very difficult for her. Finally, Stella reveals the reason for her own referral: Borderline Personality Disorder, which leads her to self-harm. Now that we know everyone they start to paint, ignoring, for now, the noise that sound like someone banging on the pipes.

From here on the play becomes a lot more interesting. Two of the group reveal that they were once patients in the hospital and give us a glimpse of life in an institution compared to 'care in the community' which is all that is available to them now. Even the Art Therapy group is under threat but, when the confrontational Stella almost causes an upset, we get the impression that the group will remain supportive of each other whatever happens in the future.

I believe that the play is good enough with the plot as described up to now but it is somewhat diluted by the banging on the pipes, old rumours of a ghost and the eventual appearance of Theresa, who has hurt herself falling off a ladder. All this seems somewhat at odds with the main story, but there is no doubt that Alison Gilmour understands this subject and has used that knowledge to create a piece of drama ideal for anyone looking for something a bit different for a festival.

THE LAST OF THE DUCHESS
Author: Nicholas Wright, from the book by Caroline Blackwood
Publisher: Nick Hern Books
ISBN NO: 9781848422063
Cast: 2 M 5F
Type: Full Length

In 1980 Lady Caroline Blackwood was employed by The Sunday Times
to play a part in what they believed would be a tremendous journalistic
coup. After Edward VIII abdicated in 1936 in order marry Wallis
Simpson, the pair became the Duke and Duchess of Windsor and began
a life of socialite celebrity, spending much of the 50s and 60s flitting
between the United States and their mansion just outside Paris. When
the Duke died in 1972 the Duchess became a recluse and was rarely seen
in public. Now the newspaper has secured the services of Lord Snowdon
to photograph the Duchess and has despatched Lady Caroline to obtain
the necessary permission and write the accompanying story.

As the play begins Lady Caroline arrives at the mansion. She finds the
Duchess approachable and a little drunk: this is not at all what she had
expected. She had been told that the Duchess was ancient and very ill:
she turns out to be sprightly and outspoken. Except that Lady Caroline is
dreaming. When she wakes up she is introduced to the Duchess's fierce
octogenarian lawyer, Maître Suzanne Blum. Lady Caroline is informed
that it will not be possible for her to speak to the Duchess. Everything
must go through the lawyer. After a brief and futile interview, during
which Blum refuses to reveal anything about the Duchess that is not
already common knowledge, Lady Caroline is dismissed, but not
before she is informed that permission for the photograph will not be
forthcoming. But Lady Caroline already has her eyes on another story.
She believes that the readers of the Sunday Times will find Blum a much
more interesting subject than the Duchess and flatters her by saying that
she will arrange for Lord Snowdon to photograph the lawyer rather than
the Duchess.

Vodka features rather prominently in this story. Blum has banned the
Duchess from having it: apparently she was just a little too fond of it.
Meanwhile Lady Caroline and Lady Diana Mosley, an old friend of the
Duchess, knock it back with abandon, resulting in them both voicing
some rather forthright opinions; though I suspect that Lady Mosley
would have quite happily voiced her opinions without the need for
vodka to lower her inhibitions.

Once the interview with Blum begins Lady Caroline becomes very interested in the lawyer's power of attorney. Could it be that the servants, including Blum, are living the high life by selling the Duchess's possessions? The famous Windsor jewels have, for some time, been appearing on the international market. Is the lawyer a thief?

Lady Caroline is prevented from publishing the story by Blum who insists on editing out anything remotely interesting. She admits that she is selling the jewels but insists that it is in order to pay for medical care. However, she tells Lady Caroline that she will sue if a word of it is printed. Lady Caroline responds that she will print what she likes, but in a book rather than in the newspaper, and if she has to, she will wait for Blum to die and then publish. She kept her word. Blum died 14 years later at the age of 95 and The Last of the Duchess was published the following year. The year after that Lady Caroline died from cancer at the age of 64.

Nicholas Wright's play is a fascinating look behind closed doors where there is a constant struggle between betrayal and loyalty; where familiarity breeds both contempt and love and how it is sometimes difficult to tell the difference between them. It is a play with characters that seem to belong to another world, and yet we cannot avoid recognising the similarities to our own lives.

It is often said that there is a shortage of plays with good roles for older actresses. Well, here's one! The Last of the Duchess is an excellent play.

THE LAST OF THE HOUSEMANNS
Author: Stephen Berresford
Publisher: Nick Hern Books
ISBN NO: 9781842422520
Cast: 3M 3F
Type: Full Length

Judy Housemann is a sixties dropout. Now in her own sixties she lives in a once beautiful art deco house on the Devon coast with celebrities for neighbours who were once friends. As she recovers from an operation she gathers her family around her and holds court wearing a Snoopy nightdress.

Nick and Libby are concerned that their mother is planning to sell the house, something they regard as their inheritance. Their father has intended to change his will, to cut out Judy all together, but he died before the solicitor arrived and Libby has noticed letters from local estate agents amongst the post.

There are some good early pointers to the type of people we are dealing with. When Libby tells her brother that she has been worried about him he replies with an infuriating "Don't be" but offers no reassurance that there is nothing for her to worry about.

Libby's daughter, Summer, is developing a teenage interest in Daniel, the son of a neighbour who comes to use Judy's swimming pool, and the cast is completed by Peter, a doctor, who seems to be interested in both Judy and Libby.

The most dysfunctional of families, the Houesmanns seem set on a path of selfdestruction; over a period of several months, through a haze of all day drinking, these leftovers from the revolutionary ideal have become trapped by their desire for a bohemian lifestyle; they have become imprisoned by the desire to be free; their pursuit of free love has cost them dear. Finally, when Judy dies, Libby scatters her ashes on the lawn. Have we really seen the last of the Housemanns?

Stephen Berresford's first play was performed by a star cast including Julie Waters and Rory Kinnear but I feel that even they must have struggled with a script that lacks direction and fails to give each of the characters a distinct voice. However, there is promise and, with the author already under commission from the National Theatre, it will be interesting to see what the future brings.

LIFE & BETH
Author: Alan Ayckbourn
Publisher: Samuel French
ISBN NO: 9780573112225
Cast: 3M 3F + 2 Voices
Type: Full Length

Christmas Eve, and the recently widowed Beth is being told by Connie, her sister-in-law, how she couldn't have done much better, as husbands go. "Yes." replies Beth, "Well he's gone now, hasn't he?" So has the cat. On the day of the funeral it went out of the cat flap never to return.

Ayckbourn himself remarked that his plays tend to follow one of two themes: extraordinary events taking place in a very ordinary setting, or very ordinary events taking place in an extraordinary setting. Given the familiar, if a little awkward, domesticity of the opening scene I think we can be assured that, before very long, something remarkable is going to happen.

First we have a visit from the vicar, a man for whom Connie seems to have something of a soft spot. Then Beth's son and accident prone girlfriend turn up. Typical family Christmas get-together tensions are in the air when they sit down for their Christmas Eve meal; then all the lights go out. A candle is lit and in the flickering light sitting in his usual place, but seen only by Beth, is Gordon, her dead husband.

In recent years we have seen only occasional glimpses of the creative imagination that made Ayckbourn our favourite living playwright and, with the interval upon us, I felt we were trundling down a well worn path.

In act two Gordon pays another visit and we learn that heaven is a more bureaucratic place than many of us would imagine and, as a retired health and safety officer, Gordon is in his element putting the other world to rights. Beth surmises that her late husband's appearance is a result of a prayer said on her behalf by the vicar and she gets him to undo it, as it were. This is only partially successful. She gets rid of her husband but it seems that she is now going to spend the rest of her days haunted by an invisible cat.

The sheer volume of plays written by Ayckbourn means that plays like Life & Beth are put at a disadvantage. It is a perfectly good play but I feel that a company deciding that they want to 'do an Ayckbourn' will overlook this in favour of one of his more celebrated plays.

LOOKING FOR LOVE
Author: Raymond Hopkins
Publisher: Hanbury Plays
ISBN NO: 9781852053292
Cast: 4M 5F
Type: Full Length

After twenty-one years of marriage James has walked out on Molly. He has already been gone for a few months when the play begins with the telephone ringing. Molly answers it. It is James. She tells him never to call again and slams the receiver down. The telephone rings again. Molly calls him a perverted pig – but this time it is the vicar on the line.

Lovers of a traditional farce will already know that they are in for their kind of evening and the dialogue is about as subtle as the humour as we are introduced to the characters and how they relate to each other. "How long have we been best friends?", "Since our school days." is typical of the no nonsense scene setting.

This best friend recommends a book to Molly: a six step miracle cure to help Molly get her life back. The first step is a trip to a health spa, giving the actress an opportunity to glam up for the next scene. Step two is to get inebriated so that all inhibition disappears. Molly doesn't seem to need a drink in order to tell her friends and family just what she thinks of them but there is comic potential in a teetotaller getting paralytic and it comes as no surprise that, once she is absolutely steaming, Molly gets a visit from the vicar.

The candid talk and drink take care of steps two and three so we start the next act with step four – kiss the first person who walks through the door. You don't need me to tell you who it is, do you? The confusion leads the vicar to believe that Molly is in love with him so, when the young man from the spa turns up fancying a fling with an older woman and with Molly's husband begging her to take him back, life has never been so complicated.

The next step is to sleep with the first man to buy her a meal and, for once, things seem to be going to plan when Molly, with reconciliation in mind, makes a date with her husband – but she is suddenly inundated with people wanting to buy her dinner. The final step – say "yes" to everything - almost ends in disaster but, at last, Molly forgets the book and gets on with her life.

As a good old-fashioned farce Looking For Love works very well. There are few surprises and I would expect the audience always to be one step ahead of the plot, but what the play lacks in subtlety it makes up for in plain old fun.

LOSING IT
Author: Derek Webb
Publisher: New Theatre Publications
ISBN NO: 9781840948462
Cast: 1M 1F
Type: One Act

Jack paces the room talking to himself about a woman whom he has loved and lost. "You're there, wherever I look." he says. Unfortunately for

Jack, she isn't. He is on stage performing a play and the actress who is supposed to be playing the part of his lost love has not turned up.

He goes off to the wings and we hear the director suggest that Jack plays both parts. Impossible, but he carries on regardless. Great fun is had as Jack struggles on, addressing the space where the actress should be, asking a question then putting up a hand and saying, "No. Don't answer that." (If only she could!), or asking, "What have you got to say for yourself?" The answer to this is, obviously, nothing.

Ad-libbing furiously Jack starts mixing his metaphors to glorious comic effect but it all becomes too much for a member of the audience. Describing Jack's attempts to do the play on his own as pathetic, she is about to leave but Jack persuades her to get up onto the stage and play the part of the missing actress herself.

There is fun as the woman struggles with the script, losing her place and misreading words, but she eventually gets into her stride. Things go reasonably smoothly for a short while but then the script of the play they are performing becomes imbecilic. Jack attempts to defend it, using a few phrases that this script reviewer intends to store away for future use, and it emerges that he is, in fact, the author.

Refusing to participate in Jack's play any longer, the woman from the audience comes up with a plan to rescue the evening. She goes off to change leaving Jack to do a couple of minutes of stand-up comedy before returning as Lady Bracknell. Jack is drawn unwillingly into performing a scene from The Importance of Being Earnest but rebels just as Lady Bracknell is about to say her most famous line. However, the woman now has the upper hand and is commanding the stage. It is all too much for Jack but, just as he is about to give up, his missing actress turns up and we are back at the beginning.

This is a very fine comedy with some wonderful moments. Derek Webb consistently produces first class scripts perfect for the amateur stage and I would urge readers to consider this or one of his other excellent plays.

LOVE IN A GLASS JAR
Author: Nancy Harris
Publisher: Nick Hern Books
ISBN NO: 9781848423176
Cast: 2F
Type: One Act

Patrick is in the bedroom of a boutique hotel near Dublin where he stands, holding his near empty glass, examining an Andy Warhol print hanging on the wall. He is joined by Eve whose opening line, "Oh my God, you've still got your clothes on!" is a joke that falls flat. It is clear that the pair are strangers and both seem nervous, but it isn't long before we discover why they are there: it is Eve's intention to become pregnant.

They have the room until noon the next day but Patrick will not be staying the night. Eve has paid for the room and has brought along a bunch of magazines to get Patrick in the mood. It isn't working. In addition to the magazines, Eve has brought a cup with a wide rim, a syringe and a catheter. She got the whole lot on eBay – there is a woman on there who sells kits.

Patrick is having second thoughts. He agreed to this arrangement when the pair hooked up on an on-line chat site but now he is not sure he wants to have a child with a woman who is so cold and methodical. Eve tells him that he is not having a child with her, she is having a child by herself: Patrick is just a donor; one of three that she has lined up.

Patrick wants to take her to dinner to get to know her, but Eve will have none of it. She has spent plenty of nights in hotel rooms with men that she loved. Now she is doing things her way.

Love in a Glass Jar is a very funny short play but never does it denigrate the tragedy of Eve's predicament. The balance of comedy and pathos is perfect and the ending is bound to leave us pondering how things might turn out for this unlikely pair. Great stuff!

LOVERS

Authors: Tony Rushforth
Publisher: Samuel French
ISBN NO: 9780573121494
Cast: 1M 2F
Type: One Act

A cemetery in Yorkshire: all grey stones and dead flowers. Maureen has steeled herself to visit for the first time since the funeral. She couldn't bear to see the new grave with the mound of earth reminding her of the coffin within. It is easier now that the ground is level and covered in stone chippings.

The grave belongs to Michael, Maureen's late husband, who died just as he was reaching middle age. Maureen already has had to cope with the loss of their only child who would have been five by now and feels that her faith is being tested.

Tending the graves is Bob. He was a father figure to Michael and it is obvious that he too feels a great sense of loss. A sombre start to a play about love and loss, but another element is about to be introduced. This is Anna, Michael's lover, and she arrives just after Maureen exits. Younger than Maureen, Anna is attractive and feisty. We learn that Michael worked in London and lived with Anna during the week. Bob knew about her and asked her to stay away. Through their conversation we learn that Maureen has been undergoing psychiatric treatment for some time. Michael wouldn't leave her whilst she was ill even though he had started a family with Anna.

We might expect passions to rise when the two women meet but it turns out that Maureen already knew about Anna. Somehow they manage to reconcile themselves to the fact that Michael lived two lives and part peacefully, neither of them aware of the strength of feeling that Bob had for Michael.

Tony Rushforth avoids being over sentimental with this melancholy play, but perhaps that is where it goes wrong. I didn't feel as moved as I should have been, given the tragedy of the story, and I didn't feel that I got to know Bob well enough to find his unspoken affection for Michael believable.

MAD ABOUT THE BOY

Author: Gbolahan Obisesan
Publisher: Nick Hern Books
ISBN NO: 9781848422681
Cast: 3M
Type: Full Length

Boy is fourteen and, according to the author's notes, the actor must be or must, without contention, resemble this age. He is black, mixed race or Asian and lives in the inner city. He tells us that his generation wants respect. Dad, in his forties, tells us that his generation had respect, whilst the third character, Man, in his late twenties, says his generation gave respect. They tell us that rules are to be followed, bent or broken, depending on the generation.

As the dialogue continues they agree, disagree, contradict, misunderstand and confuse. They question where responsibility lies and the importance of reputation. Their different perspectives highlight what has become known as 'the generation gap'; but are they so different?

The text is lyrical, almost poetic, and holds our interest through variety. At times the characters are talking direct to the audience, at other times they address each other. Their dialogue is often humorous and, at times, shocking. It is as though they are voicing their thoughts which, on the surface, can appear to be random but, as we eventually realise, are all connected.

At the heart of the story is a sexual attack on a girl that the boy allowed to happen but did not participate in. His refusal to give the names of the boys involved means that he is the only one who is punished: something that he accepts as being preferable to gaining a reputation as a grass.

The snappy dialogue means that the play has excellent pace but the enigmatic nature of the characters makes it difficult to engage with them at first. However, once we get to know them, they get under our skin and we are left hoping that maybe Dad and Boy have finally come to understand one another.

A MAD WORLD MY MASTERS
Author: Adapted by Sean Foley and Phil Porter from the play by Thomas Middleton
Publisher: Oberon Modern Plays
ISBN NO: 9781783190195
Cast: 14M 7F
Type: Full Length

Quentin Crisp described nineteen fifties Soho as the place where he lived la vie de bohème and I believe that he would have felt very much at home in The Flamingo Club where our play begins. As the band finishes playing, Dick Follywit leaps onto the stage and attempts to kiss the singer. There is a drunken brawl which ends when Follywit and his cohorts are thrown out. But Follywit is not the local hooligan that he appears to be: he is the grand nephew to Sir Bounteous Peersucker, an old and extremely wealthy knight, whose riches and influence allow Follywit to live life to the extreme.

I was pleased to find that this adaptation has kept most of the language of the original, the only changes being to aid comprehension. The authors have found a lot of similarities between London of 1608 and post war Soho where people are concerned with deteriorating morals, changes to the class system, the position of women in society, and immigration. It is in this atmosphere that Follywit is going to have to live on his wits if he is going to gain access to his uncle's cash.

The character names alone are enough to give a flavour of the often bawdy humour: there are Mr Littledick, Spunky, Sponger, Masters Whopping-Prospect and Muchly-Minted, and, my favourite, Truly Kidman, a prostitute who disguises herself as a nun in order to gain access to Mr Littledick's wife.

Although Follywit succeeds in robbing his uncle whilst also being the hero of the hour, it is the police constable that ends up bound and gagged, Sir Bounteous does not seem unduly concerned. As he observes, "Who lives by cunning, mark it, his fate's cast. When he has fooled all, then it's himself fooled last."

There is a great deal of delicious, and very rude, humour, most of it lifted directly from the pages of the original play, but the authors have put their own mark on the text making it not only relevant in the twentieth century but also extremely funny.

THE MADDENING RAIN
Author: Nicholas Pierpan
Publisher: Samuel French
ISBN NO: 9780573142147
Cast: 1M
Type: Full Length

Told as a monologue, The Maddening Rain is the story of a man, unnamed, who, though still only in his mid twenties, has already led quite an eventful life. Choosing to move to London and look for work rather than go to university he had a number of menial jobs before deciding to make use of his A levels and get something decent. He got a job working behind a glass wall in a bank and, before he knew it, four and a half years had gone by.

Then he ran into an old friend on Tottenham Court Road. Will had been to university, Cambridge no less, and now worked at Deliotte. It didn't matter that it was a junior role and that the pay wasn't very good; people showed you respect if you said you worked at Deliotte and our storyteller used Will to get himself a job with the firm. A few weeks later tragedy struck. Will was killed, murdered on a train, over an argument about Mini Cheddars.

Back at work our storyteller is little more than the tea boy but he manages to turn this to his advantage. Every day he is given £50 to fetch 15 coffees, 15 croissants and some doughnuts. He does a deal with a local café to supply them for £40 and he is making £10 profit every day. That's £2600 a year tax free!

He then gets a lucky break and is able to do one of the traders a favour. His reward is to be promoted to become a trader himself and soon he is handling millions of pounds on a daily basis. But the market has collapsed and soon there are to be redundancies. He recalls a story that Will wrote at school about a rain storm that turned people insane when the water touched their skin. One man stayed inside but couldn't reason with the others. In the end he threw himself into a puddle so that he could be like everyone else. This is what our storyteller does. He can see the insanity around him. He can see that everyone lives disjointed lives, no one connects, no one has any real friends, no one has compassion for their colleagues. The only way to survive is to be like everyone else and look after number one – whatever the cost.

This is a story told with frank honesty. There is Humour and heaps of poignancy. It might not be to everybody's taste but there is no denying that it is beautifully written.

THE MARTHA SYNDROME
Author: Scott Marshall
Publisher: J Garnett Miller
ISBN NO: 9780853436799
Cast: 1M 2F
Type: One Act

We are in a police interview room where Detective Inspector Carpenter and Detective Constable Melanie Crane are speaking to a woman that they have brought in for questioning. She was found wandering around in the park at seven in the morning and appears to be a little confused. She is not hostile, at times she is quite talkative, but she isn't answering their questions. More worrying, though, is that her hands are covered in blood, and it isn't her own.

When asked about the blood the woman becomes distressed. Her hands are not clean. She must get some water. She must clean her hands. At first she is unwilling, or unable, to tell the police her name, but she finally blurts it out. Baxter. She is Mrs Baxter and her daughter is Angela. Carpenter soon realises that the woman in front of him is the wife of the most ferocious criminal lawyer in the town. Suddenly his whole attitude towards her changes; he wants rid of her, to have her taken home and forget about the whole thing, but the young constable objects. They cannot let her go until they have an explanation for the blood on her hands.

As the tension between the two officers builds, the woman begins to display further signs of Obsessive Compulsive Disorder, or Martha Syndrome – a need always to be busy. As she does so she reveals more information about herself: the beatings that she receives from her husband; their son, Adam, who suffers from Neuromuscular Disorder, and her husband's womanising. Her assertion that Adam is now "in a safe place" alarms the police but their fears for Adam are misplaced. Her son was not her victim.

The Martha Syndrome is a well paced play offering an excellent opportunity for an actress to display a range of emotions and, whilst the end does not come as a great surprise, the author has introduced enough elements to keep an audience hooked on the story.

MEETING MISS IRELAND
Author: Rosemary Jenkinson
Publisher: Nick Hern Books
ISBN NO: 9781848423176
Cast: 1M 1F
Type: One Act

Kathy Ireland sits at her kitchen table with a pen and paper in front of her. A man, whom we later learn to be her brother Stevie, enters and she begins to question him. The questions are inane, reminiscent of beauty contest interviews, but Stevie's reply to her query about what he does for a living comes as a surprise. He tells her that he sells drugs, not for a pharmaceutical company but as a private enterprise. In short, he cultivates and sells marijuana.

Kathy is displeased. Stevie is helping her prepare for speed dating through role play and is supposed to be pretending to be George Clooney rather than answering her questions as himself. She sends him out of the room telling him to come back as Leonardo but they don't get very far as they soon begin an argument about the amount of electricity used to cultivate the said marijuana.

In scene two Kathy has been on her speed date and it went very well prompting a determination that her brother should move out so that she can bring her date home. Stevie appeals but the fact that he is now armed with a baseball bat ahead of the anticipated arrival of a man in a balaclava does not really help his cause.

Meeting Miss Ireland is a funny short play and the dialogue captures the sibling squabbling very well. It is a pacey script with, perhaps, a bit too much to take in but it brings a smile to the face despite the violent undertones.

MIND THE GAP
Author: Joe Graham
Publisher: Kenyon Deane
ISBN NO: 9780715504185
Cast: 3F
Type: One Act

We are in Club Limbo, a nightclub, with Sara, Lou and Katy: three women in their early twenties who are out 'on the pull'. In a break from the music Lou talks of her dreams of being an actress. There is an amusing role play during which she demonstrates how she had to 'break her boyfriend's heart' in order to put all her energy into pursuing her chosen career. But the others mock her, telling her that the only way she will get anywhere is by sleeping her way to the top. Lou's response is to challenge her friends to explain just what they are doing in the pursuit of their dreams.

There is more role play as they take it in turns to regress and they each reveal the difficulties they face (being) in the gap between being in education and being in employment: how age and experience make one realise that life is not as simple as it appears when one is a child.

I had some difficulty accepting the credibility of these three young women but it is a fun play, nevertheless, and one that a young cast would enjoy.

MOBY-DICK
Author: Adapted by Sebastian Armesto from the novel by Herman Melville
Publisher: Oberon Modern Plays
ISBN NO: 9781849435109
Cast: 8M
Type: Full Length

We begin with an empty stage and an acting ensemble arriving to perform a play. As the actors change out of their street clothes, one might imagine that we are about to see a play about a stage adaptation of Herman Melville's novel. They address the audience saying that Moby-Dick is the kind of book that people pretend to have read, and that this play should help them with that deception. They assure us that they all have read it – except for Keith, who is dyslexic.

So with that established, and a few practices of "Call me Ishmael", it is off we go - but the direction is downhill.
Once the story begins the ensemble abandon the tomfoolery of the opening minutes and embark on a fairly faithful recounting of the story. Although this is fine, even though it felt a bit odd after the way the play started, the biggest problem with the script is that, as I ploughed on, I became increasingly disengaged.

This play was written for a performance by a specific ensemble and was published, I suspect, to sell to audience members as they left. If I'm right then the purpose of the script is to serve as a memento to people who saw the performance rather than to enable anyone else to perform the play. For that reason, I am unable to recommend it to anyone looking for a suitable adaptation of Moby-Dick to perform on the amateur stage.

THE MOUSE AND HIS CHILD

Author: Russell Hoban adapted for the stage by Tamsin Oglesby
Publisher: Oberon Books for Young People
ISBN NO: 9781849434652
Cast: Varied. 40 Characters
Type: Full Length

Russell Hoban's The Mouse and his Child was first published in 1967 and is considered to be classic of children's literature. This energetic adaptation was first performed by the Royal Shakespeare Company at Stratford Upon Avon in 2012.

The play starts as the clock strikes twelve and a Tramp begins to rifle through a dustbin. A dolls house appears, a Monkey cycles past on a unicycle and, as the Tramp spills the contents of the bin, a collection of clockwork characters, including a ball-balancing Seal with a barcode on her bottom, come to life. A Child enters and sneezes. An Elephant blesses him and the Child asks his daddy where they are. His daddy, the Mouse, doesn't know so the Child asks what they are. The Mouse doesn't know the answer to this either so the Elephant explains. They are toys, they are in a toy shop and if people like them then they will buy them for their children for Christmas. And it will be Christmas soon.

The play is set in the present so it is no surprise that, come Christmas, the Mouse and his Child find themselves discarded in favour of remote control cars and other more exciting toys. They find themselves on the rubbish dump where Manny, a rat, appears to come to their rescue, promising to take them with him to the royal palace. The Mouse thinks Manny is teasing them but no, he is winding them up: well, they are clockwork! But Manny is only interested in the Mouse and his Child for their motors so the pair escape, facing many dangers as their journey takes them into the unknown.

Along the way their motors become rusted and, unable to move, they are scooped up by a Hawk who obviously considers them to be easy prey. However, when the Child explains that they are made of tin, the hawk drops them and they hit the ground smashing into pieces: perhaps the Child might have saved that piece of information until they were no longer in mid air!

Along comes the ball-balancing Seal with her new boyfriend, a Kingfisher, and they start to assemble the Mouse and his Child back together. The Elephant arrives with new motors and they are soon as good as new. Restored, they mount an attack on Manny and his gang, victory coming when they relieve Manny of his horrible rat's teeth. After this Manny turns over a new leaf: now dedicated to doing good, he teaches the Mouse and his Child the secret of self winding and with the Mouse and the Elephant in love, our happy ending is assured.

Like Russell Hoban's original story, there is plenty in this adaptation to please adults as well as enchant children. At one point one of the characters turns to the audience and says "pathos and comedy". I'm not sure I'd go that far but with plenty of depth to the main characters and the story moving along at breezy pace this script offers an imaginative director a challenge that could prove to be very rewarding.

MUSTAFA
Author: Naylah Ahmed
Publisher: Nick Hern Books
ISBN NO: 9871848422643
Cast: 4M
Type: Full Length

Mustafa is in prison for a crime that he did commit. As the play begins Dan, a prison officer, is searching his cell. He is looking for Kit Kats, crisps, anything. It's not right; the man never eats – he must have a stash somewhere in his cell – but Dan finds nothing except for a chalk circle drawn on the ground. Dan thinks of witchcraft. Len, a more senior prison officer tells him to "Give over!"

Meanwhile, Mustafa is in the 'goldfish bowl', a room with a large window where prisoners can meet their legal representatives. Mustafa's legal representative is his own brother, Shabir, who is saying they are going to launch an appeal. He thinks that he can get the sentence reduced; that Mustafa's previous solicitor wasn't up to the job. But mostly Shabir is angry with Mustafa for not telling him that he was back from Pakistan. He wants to love his brother but is finding it difficult.

These opening scenes do a good job of planting a seed of interest. On first impressions it is difficult to imagine that the troubled Mustafa can be guilty of manslaughter but there is obviously more to him than meets the eye. We are already anticipating conflict with Dan, but first of all it is Len who has to sort out what happened the previous day in the dining hall. Another prisoner ended up with his food tray in his face. Mustafa admits that it happened but it wasn't him: it just happened. Len is kind. He says that he wants to help, so it is a shock when he slaps Mustafa across the face.

As we delve deeper we learn why Mustafa is such a troubled soul. He believes that he is possessed by a Djinn – a supernatural spirit – that took over as he tried to exorcise the young boy that he is now in prison for killing. Now the Djinn is causing havoc. Other prisoners sustain mysterious injuries in the shower or have their trays crash into their faces in the dining room. Even prison officers execute violent actions that they cannot explain. Then, as we reach the climax, the spirit materialises first as Dan and then as Shabir. Somehow Mustafa has to find the strength to make the ultimate sacrifice.

With such a story line this play is bound to be compared to Hammer Horror films but Mustafa stands well in such a comparison. The characters are complex, the sub-plots intriguing and the cultural elements make it all the more interesting.

NEEDLE TIME
Author: Derek Webb
Publisher: New Theatre Publications
ISBN NO: 9781840948833
Cast: 2M 1F
Type: One Act

Needle Time is a radio industry phrase which refers to the amount of air time a particular record receives, but it could also mean the time to needle someone: to pester them; get under their skin – like a needle. In Derek Webb's play, Rob is a disc jockey on (cue cheesy jingle) Sunshine Radio. He is reasonably content with his life at present. He has worked at bigger stations but is happy to describe himself as an ageing hippy and enjoys the freedom he has on his late night show to play pretty much whichever records he likes.

Into this environment walks Suzie. The record she would like Rob to play is her brother's new single, but Rob is having none of it. He is dismissive to the point of rudeness and as he talks, mainly about himself and mostly untrue, it is difficult to find much to like about this arrogant and conceited man. Suzie, meanwhile, can be quite feisty herself, but she mostly grins and bares it in the hope that she will win Rob over and get her brother's record played.

For me, this play doesn't quite hit the mark. Neither of the characters are all that engaging and, though there is a bit of a twist at the end that gives Suzie the upper hand, I feel it would be more satisfying if she had played a more proactive role in bringing about this change of circumstance and that her actions had more relevance to the title of the play.

NEVER A CROSS WORD
Author: Ros Moruzzi
Publisher: J Garnett Miller
ISBN NO: 9780853436843
Cast: 2 - 6M 1F
Type: One Act

Bernard is retiring from his position as a partner in an accountancy firm. As a stickler for routine and efficiency he was always a 'somebody' at work, but now at a loss for anything else to do, he starts organising his wife, Julia.

Before her husband's retirement Julia was happy to comply with his routine: breakfast at 7.00am, jacket on at 7.13; and home at the same time every day to have the same brief conversation before supper. On the first day of his retirement Bernard is up early and wearing the same suit that he wears every Monday. He tells his wife to sit down and prepare for the first appointment of the day: breakfast meeting.

To combat her frustration Julia enters a fantasy world inhabited by dishy French waiters and smarmy Mafia bosses, whilst Bernard's decline escalates. Soon he isn't bothering to shave and is still moping around the house in his dressing gown at lunchtime. Finally Julia realises that Bernard is incapable of helping himself and it is up to her to find him a purpose in life. With a bit of freelance accountancy work and a position on the Board of Governors at the school, Bernard regains his self respect and Julia no longer needs her fantasies.

This is not the first script that I have read about a retired person trying to impose the discipline they knew at work into their home life, but Never a Cross Word is nicely written with plenty of gentle humour to appeal to an older audience.

NICHOLAS NICKLEBY
Author: Charles Dickens, adapted by Jonathan Holloway
Publisher: Samuel French
ISBN NO: 97810573113154
Cast: 5M 2F with doubling
Type: Full Length

This adaptation toured the UK in 2001 but has only recently been published, presumably to cash in on the interest generated by the 200th anniversary in 2012 of Dickens' birth.

On his arrival at Dotheboys Hall school young teacher, Nickleby, is shocked by the extent of the cruelty handed out by despotic headmaster Wackford Squeers. One boy, Smike, is singled out for unrelenting and undeserved punishment but, when Nickleby comes to the boy's defence, the ferocity of his attack on Squeers leads him to believe that he has killed the master.

Nickleby's dismay at what he finds at Dotheboys Hall comes over well but the script is unclear on why he forms such a bond with Smike. Later, whilst the pair are on their way to Portsmouth, they meet Actor-Manager Vincent Crummles who questions Nickleby on their relationship, suggesting a homosexual romance. The author chooses not to develop this theme, making me wonder why it was even introduced, and the pair soon find themselves performing in a play where the actors drop in and out of playing other characters from the main story. I found this rather confusing.

The relatively comfortable life in Portsmouth is short lived as Nickleby soon returns to London after hearing of the abuse his sister is being subjected to by his uncle. However the discovery that Squeers is still alive means that he and Smike face a precarious future.

When this adaptation toured in 2001 it was set in the 1950s, but the author has been careful to exclude anything that suggests a particular period and has remained faithful to the storyline. This means that there is an awful lot to cram in to a couple of hours and we lose the subtleties that help establish the characters in a whirlwind of action. I don't want to be too harsh, however. Nicholas Nickleby is a complex novel and Jonathan Holloway has done well to get it to work on stage.

THE NIGHTINGALES

Author: Peter Quilter
Publisher: Samuel French
ISBN NO: 978057311349
Cast: 2M 3F
Type: Full Length

We know that we are in for a gentle comedy when a play starts with controversy over the last chocolate biscuit! It is the mid fifties and we are in the home of Jack Nightingale. His housekeeper, Geraldine, has given said biscuit to Maggie who has arrived with a contract for Jack to sign. The pair are cabaret performers, though it seems that they perform more at home than anywhere else.

Jack and Maggie engage in quite delightful banter. It is engaging and teasing and it is obvious that these are people who know each other very well and have great affection for each other. To Jack's dismay he has two further visitors: his parents Charlie and Beatrice. They have arrived for what is these days sometimes called a "staycation". Despite having a perfectly good house of their own they have decided to come and stay with their son for a little while. Not long – they'll be gone by Christmas. Trouble is that it is only January 8th!

In the next scene it is the middle of the night and Beatrice emerges from her bedroom fully dressed and carrying suitcases. She is planning a midnight flit: to steal away silently in the night. But things like that don't happen in plays like this and, though she does manage to get away in a taxi, the whole family, plus Geraldine and Maggie, witness her disappearance. Beatrice, it seems, has left Charlie. They work out that she is on her way to Dover and Geraldine and Charlie set off in pursuit. Left alone Jack and Maggie have a heart to heart: she just wants someone with whom to spend the rest of her life. He thinks that this is a ghastly idea but we suspect he might change his mind before the end of the play.

The following morning Beatrice has returned – but without Charlie! She can't stand being with him anymore so if she isn't permitted to go off to France then he will have to go! But in the end everyone is reconciled and, yes, Jack does allow himself to fall for Maggie.

The Nightingales is, indeed, a gentle comedy but that is not a condemnation. It is a little unbelievable at times and will produce more smiles than hearty laughs but it is pleasing nonetheless and has a couple of good roles for older cast members.

NIGHTWATCHMAN

Author: Prasanna Puwanarajah
Publisher: Nick Hern Books
ISBN NO: 9781848422209
Cast: 1F
Type: One Act

Nightwatchman is the first play in the second volume of Double Feature which publishes four plays by young playwrights who made their débuts at the National Theatre in 2011.

Abirami is a cricketer: a young British Sri Lankan who is about to play the innings of her life. Playing for England against Sri Lanka she takes to the nets to practice against a bowling machine.

Set inside a sports hall we hear, but do not see, the balls being delivered as Abirami uses the batting practice to exorcise her frustrations, fears and dreams. She starts with her nickname: the Tamil Tiger. OK, she is a Tamil, but she isn't a tiger. She's from Eccles. Not that she believes that the person who gave her the nickname is racist; just an idiot; though she uses a stronger word than that. Then, as she begins to hit the balls more sweetly, she begins to imagine what it would be like to score a century at Lords on her début; perhaps with Mike Atherton commentating as she does so. Atherton, who held out for two days in 1995 against an onslaught from Allan Donald. What a hero!

Next, her thoughts turn to politics and terrorism two words that are eternally linked for Tamils. The ethnic cleansing that drove her family from their country and the hatred for what is happening in his homeland lead Abirami's father into saying to her, "If you're going to play cricket, you had better bloody well play for England."

The tension rises, the bowling machine sends down ever more aggressive deliveries as Abirami gets ever more angry: angry at the racism she suffers from every day, yet she would rather live in England than Sri Lanka. She would rather call herself English than Sri Lankan, so disgusted is she at the terrorism being perpetrated by her own people.

What a first play from Prasanna Puwanarajah: there is passion, rapture and rage in abundance; the concept of the drama unfolding in the practice nets brilliantly emphasising the powerful text. I would love to hear of this play being performed again. I, for one, would travel the length of the country to see it.

NINETEEN NINETY-TWO
Author: Lisa McGee
Publisher: Nick Hern Books
ISBN NO: 9781848423176
Cast: 2M
Type: One Act

The setting for this play is pretty grim. We are in a room in a run down, abandoned house in the countryside: a broken television set stands in the corner; a pile of books on the floor is directly under a noose hanging from the ceiling; but the room is dominated by a large wooden crate.

John Paul is examining his bruised face in a shaving mirror, his shirt splattered with his own blood. His brother, David – who is responsible for John Paul's injuries, is attempting to do a crossword. Finally he speaks. "Something, something, something E, something, something S."

They appear to be waiting for something but we don't know what. They bicker. They argue about the crossword; about cups of tea; and about a packet of hobnobs; but the air is full of menace. When David leaves the room to move their car to the back of the house John Paul is left on his own with the crate. There is a knocking sound coming from within.

When David returns he asks if "she", meaning the person inside the crate, has come round. John Paul remembers her words: "That wasn't me". Was she claiming that she was not the 12 year old who murdered their baby brother in 1992 or that six years in the detention centre have changed her? John Paul thinks it is probably the latter. David goes back to his crossword. "Something, something, something E, something, something S."

The casual attitude of the men to what they have done is quite chilling but I found the script rather frustrating. So much is left unexplained: why did David attack his brother; what is the purpose of the noose; who are they waiting for and why have they brought the woman in the crate here? It is all very well leaving a few things open but this script just left me confused.

NO NAUGHTY BITS
Author: Steve Thompson
Publisher: Nick Hern Books
ISBN NO: 9781848422056
Cast: 6M 2F
Type: Full Length

In 1975 Monty Python's Flying Circus was broadcast across America for the first time; but the censor cut out all the naughty bits. Steve Thompson's play tells the story of when Michael Palin and Terry Gilliam flew to New York and found themselves at the centre of a court case about freedom of expression and artistic integrity.

At first Palin is unwilling to go, his bitterness over the decision by John Cleese to leave the show and begin work on Faulty Towers very evident, citing this for the reason why the BBC had cancelled the programme and claiming that, with no money coming in, he would be better spending his time looking for work. He is persuaded, however, when he learns that, at a time when America is just latching on to Python humour, the network has cut out a quarter of the laughs.

Gilliam, an American who came to work in Britain due to the over-zealous censorship so abundant in his own country, is smarting for a fight and, when the pair arrive at JFK Airport, they find that the press have already picked up on the story. The American promoter boasts that this is going to be a landmark court case but Palin is confused. He thought that they had flown out to have a conversation with the network; not take them to court. But that isn't how things work in America. Their lawyers had already taken out an injunction against the next episode being broadcast.

As the case begins it seems simple. The network had signed an agreement that they would not make any changes to the script. But is gets complicated when the network argue that they didn't change the script: they changed the video. They say that they had to make the cuts in order to fit in the adverts, standard practice in America, but Gilliam points out that it is a remarkable coincidence that the number of minutes that they had to cut corresponds exactly to what he terms 'the naughty bits' from a scene where these were the very words cut by the network.

The arguments around artistic integrity are no match for dollars. The network claims they would lose revenue if they were unable to broadcast the advertised programme and, as a result, they win the case. This is not the end of the story however. Palin appeals and, with the appeal being heard after the programme had been broadcast, and therefore the loss of revenue argument no being applicable, he eventually wins his case.

It is not easy to be funny when writing about a factual event, even when the participants themselves are comedians, but No Naughty Bits, whilst it might not be something completely different, is an entertaining play which will appeal to an audience of a certain age to whom Monty Python's Flying Circus was a breath of fresh air.

NO ROMANCE
Author: Nancy Harris
Publisher: Nick Hern Books
ISBN NO: 9781848421615
Cast: 3M 4F
Type: Full Length

No Romance consists of three stories with a common theme. In the first we find Laura looking slightly silly in her sister's bridesmaid dress which is two sizes too small for her. She is supposed to look medieval – Knights of the Round Table sort of thing – but when she tries to enhance her look with a wand she looks even more ridiculous. She is at Gail's flat-cum-studio for a photographic shoot. Inspired by a saucy blog on the internet she wants to create a portfolio of erotic photos depicting scenes from classic literature and has turned to her old school friend, now a professional photographer, to do the shoot. Laura's motivation seems a bit obscure at first but then it all comes pouring out. She wants to give her partner a present for his birthday and thinks a set of naughty pictures of herself is just the thing. It all sounds a bit pathetic but the author has shown real skill in just getting us to the stage when we are about to condemn Laura when she reveals that she has found a lump. She has cancer. She is thirty-five and fears she is going to lose a breast.

But this is not a play about cancer or naughty pictures: it is about relationships. Laura is going doing to photos as a leaving present for her partner. She doesn't want him to have to look after her. Gail, meanwhile, has broken up with her partner and wryly muses on the nature of modern relationships. When you just live with someone there is no wedding dress to rip up when it all breaks down. No expensive present(s) to destroy. All she could do was smash a coffee cup and de-friend her partner on facebook.

If the play had ended there I would be singing its praises but there are two stories to go yet. The next story is fully of anger: mainly Joe's. He is in a funeral parlour and his anger is directed at his daughter far away in Australia. His mother lies in a coffin and the daughter is taking her clothes off and posting pictures of herself on the internet. "I hope you are happy. You've finally killed your grandmother." he tells her.

But the photos are only of her larking about in a wet t-shirt with a few friends. We soon learn that Joe's anger comes from his own sexual insecurities. In the funeral parlour, with his mother lying in the coffin, Joe's wife takes a pair of stockings out of her bag. They are Joe's. He ordered them from a website that sells used ladies' underwear to men like Joe. He denies it. It was a mistake. What is his wife doing opening his post anyway? But there is more. She has seen emails to him from women with names like Sandy and Suki and he pays for all this on his credit card. There is plenty of humour as Joe becomes increasing desperate to lie his way out of the situation but we are also reminded of the grim reality of the business of sex.

The final tale begins with Michael lowering his eighty-year-old mother, Peg, into a brand new state of the art wheelchair. His twelve year old son, Johnny, is of little help and Peg is far from happy. It isn't the wheelchair that makes her unhappy; it is why it was bought. So that she can go into a home.

With his father out of the room Peg tries first to frighten, then to bribe, Johnny into helping her out of the chair. He won't help her so instead she tells him stories no twelve year old would want to hear from his grandmother. How, as a young woman, she borrowed a pair of silk stocking from her sister as a treat for her husband but all it earned her was a punch in the face. How she once went off with her husband's best friend, Jack, and when she returned the next day she wasn't even asked where she'd been. Finally she tells of how Jack went off and married a German woman and that he was the only person that her husband really loved.

I have to admire the way the author delves into the secret lives of her characters and lays bare their fears and longings, but I could scream at her for the way the play ends. Most people would see it coming a mile off and it is such a letdown after the beautifully told stories that take us to that point.

PARLOUR SONG

Author: Jez Butterworth
Publisher: Nick Hern Books
ISBN NO: 9781848422261
Cast: 2M 1F
Type: Full Length

Parlour Song is published within Plays One: a collection that includes everything written by Jez Butterworth up to, but not including, his most celebrated work, Jerusalem. It does contain The Night Heron, which has already been reviewed in these pages, and two previously unpublished monologues. Parlour Song was first performed in New York in 2008.

We are in the suburban home of Ned and Joy. Ned blows things up for a living. He obviously enjoys his work as a demolition expert because the story begins with him playing a video to his friend and neighbour, Dale, of a cooling tower in Leeds being razed to the ground. Ned has lots of videos: he swaps the ex-cooling tower for a soon-to-be former gasworks on Falkirk Industrial Estate but Dale has to go and, besides, he has already seen it. He has also seen the erstwhile Kilmarnock block of flats. In fact, he has seen all of Ned's videos. As he is about to leave Ned says, "Everything's disappearing"; this the first hint of the darkness typical of Butterworth's plays.

Ned's possessions are, indeed, disappearing: his cuff-links, a birdbath, his lawnmower. A lawnmower that was in a shed protected by a padlock; but the padlock has been crudely forced open causing injury to the person who did it. There is blood on the padlock. Joy, Ned's wife, is wearing a plaster on her finger.

The marriage is on the rocks. With Ned away on business, Joy takes Dale to her bed. They plan to elope; to meet at midnight in the car park of the Arndale Centre before Ned blows it up, but both have cold feet and the play comes to an enigmatic end where life just goes on.

It is the little observations that make Jez Butterworth's plays special. The story behind the purchase of the birdbath reveal that Ned has an unconventional, romantic nature and his vanishing possessions are a neat simile for him losing the love of his wife. Parlour Song is a quirky little play but well worth considering.

PASTORAL
Author: Thomas Eccleshare
Publisher: Oberon Modern Plays
ISBN NO: 9781849434447
Cast: 4M 4F
Type: Full Length

Moll is in her empty kitchen eating from a packet of pre-sliced fruit. She looks out of the window and declares that everyone out there is fat. "Four fat women, two fat men, five fat children and a fat infant".

When she opens her handbag a fly flies out. Later, when she opens her compact, an ant crawls on to her hand. But it isn't just Moll's flat that is being overrun by animals. Deer are wandering the streets; there are squirrels and birds everywhere and trees are ripping through the concrete destroying the car parks; there are moles in Paperchase; a rabbit warren in Aldi. Nature is taking over. Two men, Manz and Hardy, have come to rescue Moll. The city isn't safe any more and they have come to take her on what she believes is a holiday.

The following evening a giant oak has come up through the floorboards. Moll is still in her flat with Manz and Hardy together with another family, the Plums, who seem to have moved in. They are waiting for a food delivery but Hardy tells them that no one is coming out: not even the man from Ocado.

Desperate with hunger they take to hunting but the animals are too quick for them. Hardy manages to capture a hedgehog but it is not enough between the six of them: it is barely a starter. Then, amazingly, the man from Ocado gets through but he has no food because the animals mugged him on the way. He still provides a meal, but not in the way that was expected, and not one that he is able to enjoy.

Pastoral has plenty of dark humour and the story is highly original. However, it does seem at times as though the author is being deliberately provocative. Arthur Plum is an eleven year old boy who uses very strong language, kisses Moll on the lips, smokes and asks for drugs. This would certainly be uncomfortable to watch but I am unclear on what this behaviour is supposed to be telling us. I did enjoy the script, though, and I'm sure that Thomas Eccleshare is a name to look out for in the future.

PRACTICE TO DECEIVE
Author: Norman Robbins
Publisher: Samuel French
ISBN NO: 9780573113420
Cast: 3M 5F + 2 others
Type: Full Length

Norman Robbins is famous for his pantomimes and farces including the wonderful "Tomb" trilogy, but he has also written some cracking thrillers and Practice to Deceive is no exception.

A number of gruesome murders have concentrated police enquiries in the remote Yorkshire village of Chellingford where watercolour artist Jessica rents a cottage on a farm owned by Mildred. Adrian arrives and is instantly made unwelcome by Mildred. There is a sign on the gate that says 'No Visitors' and Mildred carries a shotgun to ensure that the instruction is observed. It is a bit of a strange way to carry on when you run a B&B but Mildred is sick of seeing reporters.

But Adrian is no reporter. He explains that he is seeking his sister who has gone missing. They have connections to the area and he fears she may have become the latest victim. She has a prominent birthmark and there are reported sightings of someone matching her description. What is more, all the bodies found had some form of 'deformity' and, even though the bodies found so far have been there for many years, Adrian thinks that the killer may have returned.

Jessica then appears, distraught having just identified the latest find as one of her friends - and this body was freshly dumped. Adrian could be right. He shows her a photograph of his sister but she doesn't recognise her. Donald asks to see it. Now in his seventies and working as a farmhand he remembers Adrian as a boy, but Mildred shoos him away leaving us wondering if we have just witnessed the first clue. Before we really have time to digest this, Gavin, another farm hand, makes a knowing comment about how many bodies might still be hidden on the moor.

Add to the mix Diana Wishart, a crime writer, and her friend, Susan, who arrive to stay in the B&B. Then there's Rhoda Bradstock, whose first appearance gives everyone a fright, but the real shock comes just before the interval when we learn that Donald has hanged himself.

Or has he? Act two and intrigue piles upon intrigue as everyone becomes a suspect. Norman Robbins weaves a very tangled web as confessions and denials come thick and fast until a conclusion is reached that ties up all the loose ends in a very satisfying manner.

Practice to Deceive will certainly keep an audience on its toes as they enjoy this good old fashioned whodunit.

PRIMATES
Author: Scott Marshall
Publisher: J Garnet Miller
ISBN NO: 9780853436867
Cast: 1M 2F
Type: One Act

Wilfie has a visitor. As the owner of a not terribly successful stationery business he hopes it is a customer but his doting secretary, Miss Blenkinsop, tells him that the lady outside insists that it is a 'personal matter'.

The lady, Eunice, is shown in and we learn that she lives across the road from Wilfie and was the recipient of Splash and Puddle: two kittens produced by Wilfie's cat, Raindrop. It seems unlikely that the felines have anything to do with her visit but we have to wait to find out whilst Wilfie dictates some important letters. As he does so Miss Blenkinsop's incompetence and Eunice's insistence in giving them the benefit of her comprehensive knowledge of trivia lead to Wilfie becoming stressed. Fortunately Miss Blenkinsop is skilled at the art of massage and she administers this whilst Eunice twitters on about the capitals of various American states.

Dictation over, we begin to learn the real reason for Eunice's visit. It seems that Wilfie's cat is not the only one having kittens! In fact, as the story unfolds, it seems to be that everyone is at it – like primates. Whatever it is that Wilfie has, that women find so attractive, he seems to have in abundance.

Scott Marshall is highly skilled at writing festival-ready, one act plays and Primates is an excellent addition to his collection.

PRIMROSE WAY
Author: Ron Nicol
Publisher: Samuel French
ISBN NO: 978057313298
Cast: 3F
Type: One Act

"What're you staring at?" demands Primrose. This ageing bag lady who was once a professional actress surveys us from the folding chair that is her home on the street. "Seen better audiences in my day." she tells us.

This is an impressive start: one that grabs the attention with anticipation of what is to come. Next we meet Mother, then Primrose as a young girl and the three of them take us through Primrose's life. Mother was a professional actress and the young Primrose decides to follow in her footsteps after being told off for swearing. Mother explains that she herself is allowed to swear because she is an actress and that is enough to convince Primrose that being an actress is to be the life for her.

What follows is mainly disappointment: unsuccessful auditions, grubby encounters on casting couches and lots of nearly-but-not-quites. The actress who plays Mother will have the most fun as she impersonates a variety of characters who appear in her daughter's life. Primrose started at the bottom, her mother's success not giving her the rung up the ladder she might have expected, and sadly stayed there pretty much throughout her career; the high spot being a part in a TV soap – except that the scene was cut and all that remained of her small screen début was a brief glimpse of her ear.

Primrose Way is a touching drama with moments of gentle comedy running through it. I feel it is a little long, as though it is written to be the right length for a festival rather than for the story, but it is an interesting tale all the same.

THE PRINCE OF DENMARK
Author: Michael Lesslie
Publisher: Samuel French
ISBN NO: 9780573122095
Cast: 10 Characters + ensemble
Type: One Act

The Prince of Denmark is, of course, Hamlet and this play imagines him as a teenager; furious with his father for warmongering and frustrated at not having any real power.

Writing for a teenage cast where all the characters can be played by actors of either gender, the author has taken great care to ensure that the main characters are authentic to those familiar with Shakespeare's work whilst displaying a number of typical teenage traits.

As a broody teenager Hamlet writes poetry to Ophelia and requests a meeting in her bedchamber. She feels compelled to agree – one day she may be queen, but her brother protests that it will surely lead to ruin and she agrees instead to meet the prince on the cliffs.

Hamlet, however, has a problem. His father has decreed that he be locked in his chamber that evening. If he is to meet Ophelia he must ask his friends, Rosencrantz and Guildenstern, to play their part in a deception.

Meanwhile, Hamlet is not alone in harbouring desires for Ophelia. Ozric is aware that he has a rival but doesn't know who it is. Ophelia's brother takes advantage of this by persuading Ozric to go to the cliff that evening and remove his rival from the equation with his sword.

The not-quite-Shakespearian language in this script is a delight and audiences of any age will find plenty to amuse them. It is a brave writer who accepts a challenge to write a prequel to perhaps the greatest play ever written but Michael Lesslie has just about pulled it off with The Prince of Denmark.

QUOTATIONS ON THE MARGIN
Author: Scott Marshall
Publisher: J Garnett Miller
ISBN NO: 9780853436812
Cast: 2M 1F
Type: One Act

Duffy and Johnson are two men engaged in some kind of role playing game. Why, we are not certain, but we get the impression that this is something that they have done many times. As they play they will come across a word that they find attractive and, with echoes of Waiting for Godot, search their mental thesauruses for alternatives. This helps establish an intimacy between them, as if they are two old friends passing the time together.

But there is more to it than that. After a while it becomes clear that Johnson is subtlety using the word play to question Duffy, with particular reference to the current whereabouts of Duffy's wife. When it becomes too much, Duffy insists that he want to end the interview. "Interview?", exclaims Johnson. "We're just having a friendly chat." But it is an interview and, despite the odd amusing diversion, such as when Duffy assumes the persona of a professional footballer, Johnson is determined to get answers to his questions.

With so much of what we see on TV and in the cinema being heavily reliant on action it is good to read a clever and engaging play like Quotations On the Margin that makes such good use of language.

THE RAILWAY SIDING
Author: Jonathan Holloway
Publisher: Samuel French
ISBN NO: 9780573122293
Cast: 3M 1F
Type: One Act

The Railway Siding was originally commissioned by the BBC as a radio play. This adaptation for the stage gives a director an opportunity to create a set for multiple locations as well as two different times.

We begin in a Welsh seaside cottage, stylishly furnished in a manner that suggests that, in the author's words, "Argos is unknown in this environment." Here we find Jack, an out of work architect who has been ensconced in the cottage by his mate, Tom. He is here to produce some drawings for a new health centre; the solitude designed to help him concentrate.

At first things don't go too well, but he is suddenly inspired. With a day to go he finishes his work and catches the midnight train from Haverfordwest to deliver the drawings in London the next morning. This is where things start to get interesting. During the journey the sound effect of the train subtly changes from modern continuous track to the cluckety cluck of old fashioned lines. The guard insists that it is just an old section of track, but we are not so sure.

Jack dozes off and when he wakes there is a woman sitting opposite him. As they talk she seems to be from another age. She? doesn't understand a lot of what she? says and the way she is dressed suggests the 1940s. And why does the train now sound as though it is being driven by steam?

117

During the scene changes the author instructs that the music should be Godley and Crewe's Under Your Thumb. Perhaps the song was an inspiration for this play: the lyrics are about a man who takes a train journey and meets an enigmatic woman who changes his life. In The Railway Siding, Jack is forced to examine his own life after listening to the woman's story but, jolted back to reality on arrival in London; he is unsure of what has happened to him during the night but resolves to get his life back on track.

This is a wonderfully atmospheric and unusual one act play. A fine addition to Jonathan Holloway's growing volume of work.

RATTIGAN'S NIJINSKY
Author: Nicholas Wright
Publisher: Nick Hern Books
ISBN NO: 9781848421677
Cast: 16M 10F + extras
Type: Full Length

In 1974 Terrence Rattigan wrote a television play about the relationship between Russian ballet dancer, Vaslav Nijinsky and his impresario Sergei Diaghilev. He described it as the greatest romance since Romeo and Juliet but Nijinsky's widow opposed the play and, though she had no legal case, Rattigan asked the BBC to postpone the production until after her death.

Nicholas Wright was originally contacted to adapt Rattigan's play for the stage but as he did so became interested in the story behind the original screenplay. So his end product is largely a mixture of Rattigan's original script and Wright's imagining of the conversations between the playwright and the widow.

Initially Nijinsky's widow explains that she merely wishes to correct an error. Rattigan has depicted her as 'a calculating little minx who plans to entrap Nijinsky into marriage'. When Rattigan produces evidence to support this description she gets to the crux of the matter. Her objection is really because of the revelation of Nijinsky's homosexual affair with his impresario. Again there is evidence to support this but the widow insists that, should the production go ahead, she will denounce Rattigan himself as a homosexual.

The producer at the BBC cannot see why it is a problem. In 1974 homosexuality had been legal for many years and there can hardly be many people who don't already know of Rattigan's sexuality. But that isn't the point explains the playwright.

The coalescence between Rattigan's original play and Wright's imagining works very well, but the most interesting aspect is what lay behind Rattigan's insistence that the play must be withheld. He explains that in every play that he writes he reveals something about himself, but he also keeps something hidden. If his homosexuality were made public then there would be nothing 'under the surface'. He would be "categorised" and that would finish him as a writer.

With a huge and varied cast Rattigan's Nijinsky would be an enormous challenge to produce in both amateur and professional theatre but maybe it is time Rattigan's play, at least in this form, finally made it on to our screens.

RECIDIVISTS
Author: Matthew Clift
Publisher: Drama Association of Wales
ISBN NO: 9781908575043
Cast: 2M
Type: One Act

Two occupants of a prison cell: Frank is a hard nut. With a brutal upbringing he has developed a rough exterior and a nasty interior; Honey, on the other hand, was spoiled as a child. Pushed on to the stage he was told he was special. But the only time he felt special was when he suffocated one of his parents with a pillow.

The highly effeminate Honey is Frank's worst nightmare but, in this confined space, the pair are forced to get to know each other. Frank is the unwilling partner in a bit of word play before we have some role reversal as the pair find themselves in the trenches during the First World War with Honey as the brutal sergeant and Frank the frightened soldier. In the trenches, or in a prison cell, the men are going to have to accept each other in order to survive.

Recidivists is a short play. If you took out the extensive, and largely unnecessary, stage directions the number of pages would not extend beyond single figures and I found the characters rather two dimensional. As a result, despite the forthright language, I was unmoved by their story.

THE RIVER
Author: Jez Butterworth
Publisher: Nick Hern Books
ISBN NO: 9781848422896
Cast: 1M 2F
Type: Full Length

A man and a woman (they are not given names) are in a cabin by a river. The man is checking his fishing equipment and cannot find his priest. The uninitiated, myself included, would wonder why he would need a man of the cloth to catch trout, but a priest turns out to be a ram's horn with a leather handle. This humour helps bring a sense of the ordinary to an otherwise esoteric opening to the play.

Before long the pair are squabbling: she doesn't want to go night fishing with him; he doesn't want to look at the sunset with her; he is annoyed because she moved the table and he doesn't like the way she says "hmmm". There is tension in the air but we are not quite sure why.

In the next scene the man is in a panic. He is on the telephone to the police explaining that a woman has gone missing. He left her on the riverbank and when he came back... mid sentence we hear a woman's voice. When she enters we realise that this is not the same woman as in the first scene but there are a lot of similarities. The second woman we meet caught a fish having been helped by a poacher using pickled onion flavour Monster Munch as bait. The first also caught a fish but she managed this on her own using skills that she had hidden from the man.

As the play progresses it becomes increasingly uneasy as we become aware that we are witnessing a story that has been repeated many times. How many women have been brought back to this cabin and what happened to them? What was the man's purpose when he invited the women to his cabin? Was he looking for something? Did he find it? Typical of an author renowned for ambiguity, these questions are largely left for us to answer ourselves. If you enjoyed Jez Butterworth's most celebrated play, Jerusalem, then you will enjoy this. But not as much.

ROSE

Author: Hywel John
Publisher: Nick Hern Books
ISBN NO: 9781848422247
Cast: 1M 1F
Type: Full Length

Arthur lies in a hospital bed wired to a heart monitor. He has had a stroke and is informed of this by his daughter, Rose, whom he hasn't seen for years. Even though Arthur cannot speak it is clear that there is tension between them, but at the end of this emotional opening scene Arthur shows his affection for his daughter by pulling her head close to his own.

The set doubles as a hospital ward and a dingy bedsit and, in the next scene, we go back twenty years to begin the journey of discovery of what drove father and daughter apart. Arthur is of Middle Eastern descent but determined to bring his daughter up 'the English way'. His language and values seem to have been heavily influenced by reading Shakespeare and Dickens before he came to Britain and, though he dotes on his young daughter, he never really answers her questions about what happened to her mother and how they ended up in this bedsit.

As Rose starts to grow up she struggles with her identity. Arthur is furious with her when she puts on a hijab; he insists that she is English but the kids in the playground call her 'Paki'. Arthur's rejection of his background, his faith and even his real name, eventually turns his daughter against him. Her propensity for very strong language upsets him and in one scene she pulls out all the stops to use the most vulgar language possible. She attends the mosque and considers herself a Muslim, disappointing her father by not being the English lady that he had hoped she would grow up to be, until her defiance results in a terrible climax.

Rose is a powerful story. It is complex and has many depths. The revelations about what made Arthur the man he was mean that the play ends with emotion to match the beginning. The subject matter, and language, push at boundaries in a way that is unique to theatre. This play demonstrates how well Hywel John is developing as a writer.

ROY BROWN: UNTITLED
Author: Derek Webb
Publisher: New Theatre Publications
ISBN NO: 9781840948837
Cast: 2M 2F
Type: One Act

Roy Brown is a discontented carpenter. He has had enough of his "ridiculous" customers who have the audacity to pester him to actually do the work for which he has been paid. There must be an easier way to make money!

Inspiration comes from a night at the theatre with his friend, Jane. Roy and Jane enter the auditorium to witness, along with us, a woman called Cordelia waving a couple of bicycle lamps around on the stage. This is Performance Art and, though Roy considers it to be "utter tosh", he also recognises that it could be his chance to make lots of money.

To the great amusement of his mate Rhys, he creates his own piece of Performance Art which involves an orange, two wooden spoons, a workbench and a chainsaw. However, a failure to get the chainsaw started means that there is no performance. Undeterred, Roy turns his attentions to playwriting and creates his masterpiece: Gimlet. It has similarities to Hamlet, but with fewer Danish princes and more small holes.

Roy's big chance comes when he spots an advertisement for an art competition. The organiser is looking for something that says something about "transforming the post industrial Welsh landscape". Oh, and the organiser is Cordelia.

He ditches playwriting and takes up painting, which he immediately abandons in favour of being a potter but, come the day of the competition, the piece he submits is... well, I won't give it away but, safe to say, Derek Webb has saved his most mischievous poke at the pretentious world of art for the end.

It pleases me that Derek Webb balances his tongue-in-cheek swipes at modern art with a reference to a screen-print by Scott King called Pink Cher 2008. Roy actually appears to admire the work – even if he doesn't quite understand what the critics have to say about it.

There is much to like about this new work from the master of festival ready plays, the wordplay around Grayson Perry and his "alt-er-e-go", Claire, amused me the most, but there is glorious silliness in almost every minute of this fairly substantial one act offering.

SAVING IT FOR ALBIE
Author: Richard Harris
Publisher: Samuel French
ISBN NO: 9780573113888
Cast: 2M 2F
Type: Full Length

Grace and Albie first met more than twenty years ago whilst holidaying in Corfu. When they meet again by chance, in the London hotel where Grace works on the reception desk, they begin a whirlwind romance which results in them being married six months later. The play begins on the day of the wedding with Grace's mother, Rose, sitting alone in Albie's Manchester flat waiting for the others to return from the reception. The phone rings and we hear Albie's answerphone message: Rose's reaction to this is enough to tell us that she does not approve of her daughter's choice of husband.

Grace arrives, shortly followed by Albie who is very much the worse for wear. He has clearly been celebrating his marriage rather enthusiastically and is virtually carried into the flat by his brother, Ray. Albie is put to bed and we don't see him again until the very end of the first act.

Thankfully Richard Harris avoids the opportunity for slapstick afforded by Albie's drunken state and takes his time establishing the characters; extracting humour in a gentle comedy of errors. Ray comes over as a thoroughly decent chap and we get the sense that Rose would have preferred him as a son-in-law as opposed to Albie. Grace, however, is defensive of her new husband, happy in the belief that the most important things in life happen by chance.

This sets us up nicely for Ray to drop his bombshell. He chooses a moment when he and Grace are alone and produces a photograph from the holiday in Corfu. Grace laughs at Albie's knobbly knees and fondly remembers the time she spent with him during those two weeks. Ray tells her, "But that is me." It seems that the brother Grace fondly remembers from that holiday is not the one that she has married.

We have already witnessed some differences in opinion between Grace and her mother whom Grace describes as a "Typical Daily Mail reader", after a remark that, "In ten years time we'll all be praying to Allah in an American accent", and when Albie reappears, now sober, but hung-over, the tension really starts to rack up. We learn that Grace did not expect her mother to come to the wedding and accuses her of only coming to show her disapproval. Meanwhile Ray accuses his brother of only marrying Grace because he was afraid of being an "ageing Jack The Lad" left on his own after his girlfriends all abandoned him, whilst Grace, herself, is angry with Ray for choosing this moment to produce the photograph believing that his intention was to "create an atmosphere".

The clever thing is that, whilst we have been anticipating all this tension, the people we expected to be at loggerheads, Grace and Albie, are about the only ones who remain on good terms though, as the play comes to an end, we expect that their marriage may be a bit of a rocky road.

This is a great play from an accomplished author. There isn't a lot of action – all that really happens is that Grace swears a bit and the pretence of polite amiability slips for a short while – but because we have got to know the characters we care about them and I can imagine that, in the bar after the performance, the audience will be discussing the relationships long into the night.

SEX AND GOD
Author: Linda McLean
Publisher: Nick Hern Books
ISBN NO: 9781848423008
Cast: 5F
Type: Full Length

Four women from different periods in the twentieth century talk about their experiences. They are on stage together and talk across each other; their stories interwoven. Sex, or rather the consequences of sex, unites them and, though attitudes have changed across the century, each of them had to give up something. In reverse chronological order the four women are:

Fiona, a skint student, the first in her family to go to university, is angry with her bank. They won't let her have the last pound in her account without closing the account and she needs it to buy potatoes to feed her hunger.

Lizzie also knows what it is like to be poor. She is constantly robbing Peter to pay Paul or asking people to "come back tomorrow" when her husband will have given her some money. She would love to get a job herself but he insists that he is the bread winner; he stays in a job that he hates to keep a roof over their heads.

Sally is trying to better herself. She is working hard to get on in her profession in order to become independent and escape her violent partner.

Jane is a pioneer. The first of her family to move to the big city to find work: she is a kitchen maid.

The ordinariness of their stories is what makes them compelling: the tales might be ordinary in the great scheme of things but they are vitally important to the women and, though the four of them have no relationship with each other, they have shared experiences.

What makes this play stand out is the form in which it is written. The women never speak to each other so it is as if they are delivering monologues but it works extremely well: it is like a piece of music where four instruments are each playing their own tunes but work harmoniously together. This is a stylish play from a writer who is not afraid to try something new.

SEX WITH A STRANGER
Author: Stefan Golaszewski
Publisher: Nick Hern Books
ISBN NO: 9781848422551
Cast: 1M 2F
Type: Full Length

Adam and Grace, a pair in their early twenties, have met in a nightclub and are now waiting for a bus. The conversation is stilted, largely meaningless and full of intensifiers: amazing, wow, mad! They take a short bus ride and, before heading to a kebab shop because they are "starving", they kiss. It is cold, lustless and uncomfortable.

The play rapidly shifts backward and forward in time; Adam preparing to go out, Adam and Grace in a taxicab, Adam's girlfriend, Ruth, ironing his shirt for him, Adam and Grace in the nightclub, drinking shots in Grace's kitchen. We know where we are heading but, before that, a glimpse into the future. It is Grace's wedding day, she is about to marry Paul and, in a speech, she explains that she had to kiss a lot of frogs before she met him.

Act two and the action concentrates on Adam and Ruth: the domesticity of their lives together, how they met and the circumstances that led to Adam's act of deception. What becomes clear is that his liaison with Grace wasn't purely accidental; he had set out to have sex with a stranger that night.

The story the play tells is not at all remarkable but the way it is told makes it interesting. The stop, start action and the blackouts, even when the action is virtually continuous, emphasise the disjointed lives of the characters. There isn't much of a plot and none of the characters are particularly likeable but Sex With a Stranger works because of its use of the presentation opportunities that are only available in live theatre.

SIDE EFFECTS
Author: Eric Chappell
Publisher: Samuel French
ISBN NO: 9780573114212
Cast: 2M 3F
Type: Full Length

In the visiting room at a private convalescent home we meet residents Frank and Paul. Frank is suffering from a rare debilitating illness that means that he has trouble lifting things and can no longer climb the stairs at home. As a result, when he is at home, he is forced to sleep in the study and his wife, June, says that she wants him back. Frank suspects that the truth is that she just wants the study back. In these opening moments we get the impression that we are going to rather like Frank, and June sounds as though she has quite a sense of humour. When Frank told her to put him out with the rubbish her response was to ask if it should be the brown or black bin. The significance of whether it should be landfill or re-cycling is, perhaps, not lost on Paul who, after Frank has made quite a few disparaging remarks about the clergy, takes off his scarf to reveal a dog collar.

But we soon learn that Paul is not a clergyman at heart. Literally. He has had a heart transplant and there is a young lady, Tracy, who is convinced that his heart once belonged to her recently deceased boyfriend, if you see what I mean. Paul's behaviour is certainly out of character.

He is swearing, smoking, drinking and has a sudden desire to buy a motorbike. He is acting much more like Tracy's dead boyfriend than a respectable vicar. But is it the heart that makes him behave this way or Tracy's influence?

Eric Chappell is a very accomplished writer with a lot of hits behind him including, of course, Rising Damp, but I have felt his recent efforts have been a bit below par. I'm delighted to say that he is back on form with this play. There is plenty to amuse with some satisfyingly clever comic moments. I loved it when Tracy finally accepted that her boyfriend had, after all, gone to a better place: Tunbridge Wells. Side Effects is a nice, compact little play and, though I could swear I could hear Rigsby's voice from time to time, I'm sure the audience will soon warm to the characters.

SILENT NIGHT

Author: Colin and Mary Crowther
Publisher: Samuel French
ISBN NO: 9780673122361
Cast: 3M 2F
Type: One Act

It is Christmas Eve, 1940. An air raid siren moans in the distance as a family creep toward their Anderson Shelter. There's Wilf, his wife, Rose, their son, Jack and, eventually, their daughter, Lily. It isn't a very good Anderson Shelter: Wilf is an engineer, not a builder, and, although the instructions issued by the government said to dig three feet down, the hole was already filling with water at one foot so that is as far as Wilf went. As a result the shelter doesn't feel very secure.

Suddenly there is a terrific explosion, very close, then silence. Lily wonders why they can't hear the "all clear" and her father calmly explains that it is because they are all dead.

Funny the things you worry about when you are dead: the fact that the disliked Aunty Jean will inherit everything because you never got round to making a will, the state the house is in because there wasn't time to tidy up, and that the ironing is still piled up waiting to be done. As they wait to be admitted into heaven a few home truths start to emerge such as where Wilf disappears to on a Saturday afternoon when he is supposed to be at the football and the distance Rose puts between herself and all others, including her husband. They appear to be a pretty dysfunctional family.

Still they wait and they reveal what they got for each other for Christmas when all that any of them really wanted was a second chance. Then Rose tells her story – something that happened when she was a child that has made her the way she is now: how she gave evidence that led to a man being hanged and how, after a brief period of celebrity, all her friends turned against her, worried that she couldn't be trusted to keep a secret.

Finally the family become reconciled and ready to meet St Peter; except that when the knock comes it isn't St Peter, but Uncle Peter from next door telling them how lucky they all are to have survived a blast in an Anderson Shelter that wasn't built correctly.

Silent Night is written to be a heart warming tale of an ordinary family in extraordinary circumstances, but it doesn't quite work. I couldn't understand why they so readily accepted the fact that they were dead and as a result I never really believed in their characters. Based on a true event, I can't help thinking that the reality was very different from what is on the page.

SIXTY FIVE MILES
Author: Matt Hartley
Publisher: Nick Hern Books
ISBN NO: 9781848422568
Cast: 4M 4F
Type: Full Length

Sixty-five miles is the distance between Hull and Sheffield. It is the distance between Pete and a person that he has never met – his daughter.

Pete has spent the last nine years in prison. Now he arrives at the family home with a pitifully small trolley case and a determination to seek out his daughter. The sole occupant of the house is now Pete's bother, Rich, but everything is just how he remembers it: right down to the stain on the carpet. The relationship between the brothers is both distant and familiar; the type you only get with people who have grown up and grown apart together.

Pete hardly knows where to start looking. Sheffield has changed so much whilst he has been away. It is a city that has been given a second chance. Will he be so lucky? Rich is also coming to terms with personal loss. His girlfriend left him after a mutual decision to abort their baby. Long before this, when he and Pete were children, they both , due to

Pete's disruptive behaviour, lost the chance for a good man to become their stepfather.

Meanwhile, Pete finds himself sitting on a bench outside a school when a fifteen-year-old girl approaches. He believes her to be his daughter – why else would she come to speak to him? Somehow she must have been drawn to him. But truth is that she is doing it for a bet, her friends sniggering in the background whilst she talks to 'weirdo'.

Eventually Pete gets an address for his daughter, and makes the sixty-five mile trip to Hull. The closest he gets to her is a conversation with her stepdad, but somehow it is enough. Knowing something about her is enough to allow Pete to move on.

Sixty Five Miles is described on the script cover as a play that ties a family together but, for me, it is equally about what pulls them apart. All the characters have lost something but, although they blame each other, they also are forced to recognise that they have to take some responsibility themselves. The play feels like a TV drama except that it is too long to hold the attention of a TV audience and would benefit from a bit of trimming for the theatre as well.

SMACK FAMILY ROBINSON
Author: Richard Bean
Publisher: Oberon Modern Plays
ISBN NO: 9781840023732
Cast: 3M 2F
Type: Full Length

In 1982, whilst at the top of his game, Adam Ant responded to media speculation about what might lie behind his apparently clean-living lifestyle with the single Goody Two Shoes which includes the line, "You don't drink, don't smoke, what do you do?" This has nothing to do with the play that I am supposed to be reviewing except that the author, Richard Bean, is currently at the top of his game with his adaptation of The Servant of Two Masters currently wowing audiences on both sides of the Atlantic as One Man, Two Guvnors and that Gavin, in Smack Family Robinson, is asking a very similar question of his daughter, Cora.

The Robinsons have a family business and, though times have changed since Gavin started it back in the sixties, it is still all about cash and stock: the products have changed but the market is still there if you move with the times. Like many family businesses the older members rely on the younger generation to keep pace with modern trends but, for the Robinsons, this is where they have a problem. Sons Sean and Robert have embraced the business but not Cora. The business, I should explain, is drugs. To put it bluntly, the Robinsons are drug dealers and Cora doesn't drink, doesn't smoke and, more to the point, doesn't do drugs.

As the play begins Gavin is watching his brand new, wide screen, high definition television with his wife, Catherine, who comments that the technology is wasted on the nature programme that they are watching - penguins are black and white! Son, Robert, arrives and, whilst being chastised for walking on the new shag pile with his shoes on, he tells his parents that his wife, Pammy, has died. This apparently devastating news is met with indifference from his parents who even start cracking jokes about it as Robert tells his sister; though to be fair, Robert doesn't seem especially distraught himself.

This is not a new play from Richard Bean, it was first performed in 2003, so it must have been quite shocking to audiences who had not yet witnessed television programmes like Shameless where the casual attitude to crime and drug abuse is a regular source of humour. However, whilst Shameless has its moments of pathos, with Smack Family Robinson it is comedy all the way; Gavin, in particular, punning with almost every line. We eventually learn that Pammy was murdered by Catherine because the 'smack head' was pregnant with Robert's child and Catherine didn't want the bother of a baby that she would probably have to bring up herself. This results in Catherine herself being murdered and, as an example of the humour, the family are much amused after the funeral to find that they are drinking de-caff (De-Cath) coffee.

Occasionally the humour is a bit more refined - I enjoyed an observation that if the Samaritans really cared surely they would ring you - but I believe that the play as a whole lacks the sophistication to be called black humour and, with a plethora of corny puns around such tragic subject matter, many will find it uncomfortable viewing.

SNOW WHITE & THE SEVEN DWARFS
Author: Simon Rayner Davis
Publisher: Spotlight Publications
ISBN NO: 978190737386
Cast: 3M 3F plus 10 others
Type: Pantomime

Many years ago I had a friend who got a job as an Assistant Stage Manager at Nottingham Playhouse. One of his first duties was to get on the front of house P.A. system to advise the audience that the performance was about to commence. He nervously cleared his throat, switched on the microphone and with his best public-speaking voice began "Jadies and Lentlemen". This panto from Simon Rayner Davis begins in similar fashion with the prologue giving us the background to the story before we get going in traditional fashion with a chorus of villagers singing the first song.

Before we know it, the independently minded mirror is being too honest for its own good and the queen is in a rage because she is no longer the fairest of them all. That title now belongs to her step-daughter, Snow White, whom she has taken to the woods where her faithful but incompetent servants, Scratch and Sniff, have been instructed to kill her. Snow White escapes with the help of several bears. This gives the audience the opportunity to shout "behind you" whilst Sniff and Scratch get confused about "bare behinds"!

Although, for the songs, the author has elected to provide new lyrics to popular songs such as Is This The Way To Amarillo and I'm A Believer, adults in the audience will be happy to join in with the dwarfs in a rousing Heigh Ho to get act two under way. The queen has to take matters into her own hands and feeds Snow White a poison apple but this is panto so Snow White will get her prince and the queen will get her comeuppance.

There is a reason why pantomimes follow a formula and that is simply that it works. Everyone but the youngest members of the audience knows the story and they will know most of the jokes: that is half the fun. Simon Rayner Davis has sensibly kept things simple and produced a script that has the perfect balance of originality and tradition.

THE SOCIABLE PLOVER
Author: Tim Witnall
Publisher: Samuel French
ISBN NO: 9780573142307
Cast: 2M
Type: Full Length

For those amongst us who have never been inside a bird-watchers hide this is what a typical one looks like: dirty and dilapidated with gaps in the timber that let in the wind and rain. On the wall a chalk board for 'recent sightings' and on the floor empty crisp packets, beer cans and discarded porn magazines.

Into this environment walks Roy Tunt. Shabbily dressed and old before his time, he dons a pair of rubber gloves and sets about making the place respectable. Satisfied, he sets out a few possessions including, in pride of place, a framed photograph of his ex-wife, Pumpkin. He turns on the radio receiver/transmitter and settles down. Having already recorded all 567 bird species on the British list in his grubby notebook he has come here in perfect weather conditions to catch a glimpse of the rare and beautiful Sociable Plover.

Roy Tunt sits and talks to himself. He is a quirky, amusing, all-right-in-small-doses type of chap but, as he waits for the voice of his friend to come out of the radio the solitude is broken by the arrival of Dave, a good looking stranger who crashes into the hide.

After some initial hostility the two strike up an unlikely friendship. Roy's natural good nature coming through as he enthuses about his hobby. Dave claims to be staying with a friend in the village; his early morning walk a cure for his hangover. But something isn't right and the tension builds as we wait for the penny to drop.

There is, however, a great deal of humour wrought from the pair discussing everything from garden gnomes to the merits of power tools which only ends when Dave goes out to answer a call of nature and the radio crackles into life with the voice warning of a police man hunt.

Strangely, Roy doesn't seem terribly alarmed by this and, before long, everything is turned on its head as we learn the truth about this unlikely pair.

With humour and pathos in equal measure, not a single word is without significance in this beautifully crafted two hander from Tim Witnall. Thoroughly recommended.

ST NICHOLAS
Author: Conor McPherson
Publisher: In Plays One from Nick Hern Books
ISBN NO: 9781848422216
Cast: 1M
Type: Full Length

St Nicholas is a monologue for an actor in his fifties. A tale of a theatre critic who gets himself caught up with a bunch of modern day vampires, the story begins with the performer telling us not to believe any of the rubbish we might have read about vampires in works of fiction. The real thing is very different.

This theatre critic seems to be exactly as we imagine. His talent does not extend beyond the ability to string a few words together. He has no ideas of his own; he is just a failed playwright who makes up for his own lack of ability by pouring scorn on the works of others. He admits to all of this.

After one show he stays for a party. He tells the director that he had loved it: had given it a fabulous review. But he is lying. He panned it and is now enjoying the appreciation of everyone involved, knowing that they will learn the truth when the papers come out in the morning. He derives great pleasure from this but feels the first pangs of guilt sharing a taxi with Helen, a rather desirable actress, on the way home.

Because of poor reviews, not just his own, the show closes early but does transfer from Dublin to London. One drunken night he flies to London to visit the director and to claim that his editor had changed his story. The cast and director are sharing a house and the critic's motivation is to see Helen again but no one seems to accept the new lies he tells them. He is offered a sofa for the night and, waking from his comatose sleep, he creeps up to Helen's bedroom but reason gets the better of him and he walks out into the night. This is when he meets his first vampire.

Michael, the vampire, gives the critic a home but, in return, he must go out each evening and bring back a group of young people for the vampires to feed off. They will not die: the vampires only take what they

133

need, and to make his mission possible the critic is instilled with natural charm. He does what is required of him but he soon tires of this life and wants to go back to Dublin to start again. The inspiration comes when he stumbles across Helen on one of his night time perambulations.

The most interesting aspect of this story is the comparison of the fantasy world of vampires to the self pitying reality of a critic's existence. In fact, there really isn't a great deal of difference. In both cases he is just doing what is expected of him, seemingly incapable of getting out of the rut that he has made for himself. But there is hope. Whether or not the vampires were real or just a dream, the critic resolves to sort his life out. Whether he will is another matter.

It is difficult to imagine that there will be many performances of this play on the amateur stage, but there is no doubting Conor McPherson's skill at storytelling. His ability to search deep into the soul of his character is remarkable, making St Nicholas a very worthwhile read.

STRANGERS MUST BEWARE
Author: Richard Hills
Publisher: New Theatre Publications
ISBN NO: 9781840948684
Cast: 4M 2F
Type: One Act

Strangers Must Beware is a wartime romance set in a small cottage on the border between Italy and Switzerland in 1944. An eighteen year old peasant girl is cooking when she hears whistles outside. Her father enters and tells her to close the curtains: it will be German soldiers searching for someone and they must not get involved. Shortly after this the father goes out and an English airman bursts in, dazed and covered in blood. His hallucination, that he is still in the aeroplane being shot down, is a bit of an obvious way to explain what has happened and, I think, could have quite easily been left to our imagination, but he is soon sufficiently compos mentis to hide under the table when German officers arrive.

After a quick search they are gone but they are back moments later when the father returns. The girl thinks that her father has betrayed the Englishman but he had been for reinforcements represented by a woman freedom fighter who arrests the Germans and allows the Englishman to escape.

Scene two is three years later. The Englishman returns to the cottage looking for the girl he has not been able to forget. Work is found for him on the farm and marriage soon follows.

The pace throughout is frenetic, which certainly conveys a sense of urgency at the beginning of the play but would, I imagine, become a bit too much for the audience to take in with entrances and exits coming quicker than in a French farce. Some of the dialogue, particularly that at the beginning of the second part, is rather unnatural: it tells the story of what has happened in the intervening years but is unlike any conversation I can imagine happening in real life. I feel that the problem is that the author has tried to cram just too much into the story and would have done better to have had less story and more depth.

STRANGERS
Author: Colin and Mary Crowther
Publisher: Samuel French
ISBN NO: 9780573122651
Cast: 1M 2F plus voice
Type: One Act

A dilapidated jetty stretches out over stagnant water. On the landing stage a fisherman silently waits for a catch. A riverwoman approaches. Not seeing the fisherman, she steels herself to go along the jetty to the water's edge. Then fear grips her and she retraces her steps.

An enigmatic start and this continues once the dialogue starts. The woman has earned her name because she owns the land, not the river, she says, because the water owns itself.

She hates it here. Her husband freed her from life at home but chained her to a life here. Now that he is dead, and her daughter is a stranger, she has moved to the city to be amongst people. We learn that she is here to hand over the keys to her house to the new owners. Her daughter, the stranger of the title, arrives and the pair fight.

But the fisherman brings about a reconciliation. He forces them to talk about Wendy, the stranger's daughter, who drowned whilst her grandmother was supposed to be caring for her. With the fisherman's help they finally start to come to terms with what happened.

A story of love and forgiveness, Strangers will tug at the heart strings and provides an opportunity to explore the depth the authors have given their characters.

THE STUBBS
Author: Steve Harper
Publisher: Samuel French
ISBN NO: 9780573122552
Cast: 3M 3F
Type: One Act

Be careful what you wish for. This is the moral behind Steve Harper's new play that was first performed in 2012. I mention that this is a new play because it has an old fashioned feel to it. Even the names of the main characters: Bill, Edith and their daughter, Violet, seem to be of another age, though the play is set in the present. Curious!

The Stubbs is an eighteenth century painting. A small gilt framed picture of George Stubbs' most popular subject: a racehorse. It was believed to have been destroyed in an air raid in 1944, but here it is hanging on Bill's wall. When Bill tells Violet's new boyfriend of how he came to acquire it there is scepticism, but also an inkling of opportunity.

The boyfriend just happens to work at an auctioneers and knows a few people, including one person who might be prepared to buy the painting, no questions asked. The deal is done during which time Bill goes from being innocently naive to manipulatingly cunning and we finally learn the reason why the family have such incongruous names.

There is a whimsical humour running through this play and this, combined with a few satisfying twists in the tale, should keep an audience pleasantly amused for half an hour or so.

THE SWALLOWING DARK
Author: Lizzie Nunnery
Publisher: Josef Weinberger
ISBN: 9780856763328
Cast: 1M 1F
Type: Full Length

Canaan arrived in the UK five years ago and was granted refugee status after he escaped with his son from violent oppression in Zimbabwe. He felt he was now safe but his leave to remain has expired and, because he has failed to fill in the necessary forms, he has been appointed a new case worker who will review his case.

Even though the process of this review makes him feel like a criminal, Canaan is articulate and demonstrates high intelligence in his answers but when asked to explain his reasons for seeking asylum he is afraid of falling into a trap. He cannot remember what he said five years ago so he is worried that if his story differs in any way it will look like he is not telling the truth. There are so many reasons for him fleeing the country of his birth it is possible that the reasons he speaks of this time might not match what he said before. On top of this his case worker, Martha, makes him feel like he needs to perform. Does his whole future depend on whether he is able to move Martha with his story?

Meanwhile, Martha has her own demons to face. Her brother is responsible for beating another boy on a drunken night out and, whilst she tries to come to terms with how her brother could use such violence on another person, she listens as Canaan confesses to being an official in the Mugabe regime and to torturing his countrymen.

In flashbacks the actress playing Martha becomes Nomsa, Canaan's wife, and we witness scenes of both tenderness and terrible violence. Canaan tells of how he was beaten and how he was forced to watch as his wife was murdered - but there are gaps in his story. Martha does what she can; she believes that Canaan would be in danger if he returned to Zimbabwe, but she cannot change the decision that he is to be deported.

I will admit that I didn't expect to enjoy this play when I picked up the script but I was gripped from the start. One cannot help be affected by the story. This is a play that forces us to accept that few of us are wholly good or wholly bad and to consider what we would do if presented with the choices that faced Canaan.

SWALLOWS AND AMAZONS
Author: Arthur Ransome, adapted by Helen Edmundson. Songs by Neil Hannon
Publisher: Nick Hern Books
ISBN NO: 9781848422377
Cast: 5M 7F
Type: Full Length

John, Susan and Titty are sitting around a camp fire when Roger rushes in with a telegram from Daddy. John reads it: "Better drowned than duffers if not duffers won't drown." The children are excited; the message means that they have permission to sail on their boat, Swallow, and set up camp on an island in the lake.

Helen Edmundson's stage adaptation of Arthur Ransome's much loved children's story set in the Lake District is remarkably effective. The children's excitement is bound to be shared by the audience so it is highly appropriate that, when the children whistle for the wind, a distinct breeze is felt in the auditorium.

With the wind behind them the children arrive on the island to find signs that someone has been there before them. Barbarians perhaps? Soon they have an answer when they spy another boat, the Amazon, with its crew of pirates! They set off in pursuit, confident that the Swallow can outrun any boat, but they have to turn back when they remember that they haven't had lunch yet and besides, they promised to let Mother know that they had arrived safely.

They pay the price for their delay. The pirates steal their boat and occupy their camp. But children are children and soon they are all pals. The Amazons are Nancy and Peggy. Well, Nancy's real name is Ruth but that is no good because everyone knows that pirates are ruthless. An allegiance is formed and together they vow to defeat the evil Captain Flint – a man occupying a houseboat who, in reality, is just after a bit of peace and quiet so he can write his book.

Children may be children but pirates are pirates and the Swallows find themselves double-crossed. This means war and, after a stormy night on the lake, the Swallows are victorious. However before they can celebrate they have a visitor; a policeman who tells them that the houseboat has been broken into and the book has been stolen. The Swallows clear their name by solving the mystery themselves and our story ends with everyone playing along, Captain Flint and Mother included, and the promise of many more adventures to come.

Helen Edmundson has brilliantly captured the innocence and good natured fun of the original and I raise a cup – sorry, I mean flagon - of lemonade – I mean rum – to her and the talented Neil Hannon for bringing the story to new generations of children and adults.

TABLE
Author: Tanya Ronder
Publisher: Nick Hern Books
ISBN NO: 9781848423282
Cast: 4M 5F
Type: Full Length

Nine actors play twenty three characters over six generations in a story that has a piece of furniture at its heart. Like Tim Firth's The Safari Party, that piece of furniture is a table, but Tanya Ronder's play is more about value than profit.

We start in the present day with nine year old Su-Lin saying that she does not want this table that she will inherit. It is "cacked up" and she wants a big glass one from IKEA instead. But her grandfather tells her that each of the "cacks" has a story behind it. And so we begin.

From the harsh realities of Victorian Britain, through the stifling atmosphere of an African convent and the rebelliousness of a sixties hippy commune, we travel back and forth, examining issues around identity and the sense of belonging. Su-Lin is the only person who I believe to be valued by those around her, perhaps because she didn't come easy; her father employed the services of a surrogate mother so that he and his male partner could have a child.

Su-Lin's grandfather is Gideon, the result of a liaison between a nun and a gamekeeper but brought up in the hippy commune when his mother was banished from the convent. He abandoned Su-Lin's grandmother shortly after their son, Su-Lin's father, was born and seems to have struggled to find his own sense of belonging ever since. Now he is back wanting to be a father to his forty year old son.

At the front of the script there is a family tree which I found indispensable with there being so many characters and time periods. This gives me cause for concern because I believe that an audience would, at times, have trouble with comprehension. This, combined with the fact that there is no dramatic climax, could leave an audience bemused, but the sheer volume of the stories behind the "cacks" on the table will give them plenty to talk about after the show.

THERE IS A WAR
Author: Tom Basden
Publisher: Nick Hern Books
ISBN NO: 9781848422209
Cast: 18M 6F
Type: Long One Act

The second play in the second volume of Double Feature is described as a miniature epic. In There is a War, Tom Basden unleashes his sense of the absurd as Non Combat Personnel are parachuted into a war zone to assist The Blues in their battle against The Greys.

After their dramatic entrance the newcomers are subjected to bureaucracy as they are challenged over having the correct paperwork and, as the story develops, the humour continues much in the same vein. There is a torturer who complains of RSI, soldiers in the battlefield who stop for lunch and a 'friendly firing squad' who deal with matters of insubordination.

Eventually a civil servant arrives to announce that the war is over and hands everyone a certificate. That is not quite the end though; we de-camp to a hospital where the wounded from both sides are being treated but a shortage of supplies leads to conflict and soon two sides emerge: The Reds and The Oranges. There is another war.

There are some nice moments in Tom Basden's script but nothing is dramatically original which makes for an entertaining but not terribly memorable play.

THICKER THAN WATER
Author: Ben Humphrey
Publisher: Drama Association of Wales
ISBN: 9781908575005
Cast: 1M 1F
Type: One Act

It is late at night and the door buzzer in Robert's flat sounds in the dark. Robert enters and presses the intercom to hear a woman, Fiona, asking to be let in. Her car has broken down, her mobile is flat and she needs to call the RAC. He tries to get rid of her but she is persistent and he eventually relents and lets her in.

Whilst waiting for the breakdown service they can chat over a cup of tea. Fiona is bright, bubbly and very beautiful. Robert is clearly attracted to her and, fortunately for him, when she goes out to meet the man from the RAC she leaves her mobile phone behind. He has an excuse to see her again.

To Robert, bored with his job and with life in general, Fiona seems like a breath of fresh air. A few months down the line, Fiona has moved in and Robert is on a roll. Things are looking bright and when she tells him that she is pregnant he is euphoric. He has just been talking about a relationship that he ended twenty two years earlier when Sophie, his partner at the time, told him that she was having an abortion. Now he is finally to become a father.

The twist is that Sophie didn't have an abortion. She went through with the birth and the child grew up to be Fiona. Robert has been sleeping with his own daughter and she has been manipulating him in order to exact revenge for what she sees as abandonment.

Thicker Than Water certainly has shock value but I found it somewhat unconvincing. There is a fine line between leaving things open to interpretation and implausibility. I fear this play falls on just the wrong side.

THE TOBACCO TIN
Author: Richard Rowe
Publisher: Drama Association of Wales
ISBN NO: 9781908575050
Cast: 2M 4F with Doubling
Type: One Act

I cannot recall the last time I sat on a park bench. They seem to be a most underused piece of furniture; I pass several when I am walking my dogs but they are rarely occupied. It is a different matter in the world of theatre, however. So many plays seem to be set around park benches that theatrical open spaces must throng with characters with stories to tell.

In The Tobacco Tin we find Arthur waiting his weekly rendezvous with his friend Dai for whom the park holds memories. We know this because Dai's first line on arrival is "This place brings back memories", to which Arthur replies, "We come here every week." This is Richard

141

Rowe's first play and, although I try to avoid discouraging new writers, I'm afraid to say that this unnatural dialogue continues throughout the script. It tells a story but it is difficult to imagine two old men who have known each other most of their lives actually talking to each other like this. I also have a problem with some of the language during flashbacks. Would a seven year old in 1940 refer to Hitler as "that German guy"? Unfortunately, as with other scripts I have received from Drama Association of Wales, there are also a number of typographical errors.

As the play develops we learn a little more about Arthur and Dai. They are just ordinary people with ordinary memories and, whilst the story is not terribly original, it is quite touching. Having the same actors playing their characters at different stages of their lives, combined with two actresses playing four roles, shows imagination and I hope that Richard Rowe continues to write for the theatre.

TOP OF THE MOURNING
Author: Scott Marshall
Publisher: J Garnett Miller
ISBN NO: 9780803436904
Cast: 5M 7F
Type: One Act

Described as an 'Irish romp' Top of the Mourning is set in the home of the Widow Quinlan where a motley collection of mourners are gathering to pay their respects. Inspired by characters from contemporary Irish theatre Scott Marshall has created a fast paced comedy where dialogue is king.

Everyone gets the chance to amuse but the best of the early lines belong to the Mayor. His terrible twinges that "does be in me right leg" (as he taps his left) are transferable "from one part of the anatomical to another" and they "obstructify" him from being the man of action that he once was.

Then there is the confused Stone McBroot who goose-steps, John Cleese style, around the room whenever anyone mentions whisky and explains his condition as being the result of a beating he once received from a sly Brit from Slough, Bucks, who pulverised him whilst singing Raindrops Keep Falling on my Head.

With so much going on this is the sort of play that audiences are going to want to see a minimum of twice to catch up on the jokes they missed the first time round. Well executed and very clever wordplay combines with daft surrealism until we reach a climax when the mention of old farmer McDonagh prompts the line "You said that farm is worth some bucks" and the whole cast join in with "Eee-eye-eee-eye-ohh".

Top of the Mourning is a great play: it is silly; it is glorious; it has to be seen to be believed.

TRAVELLING LIGHT
Author: Nicholas Wright
Publisher: Nick Hern Books
ISBN NO: 9781848422476
Cast: 10M 3F + 6M 3F on film
Type: Full Length

At the turn of the twentieth century in an Eastern European village the 22 year old Motl Mendl makes an exciting discovery. Amongst the effects of his recently deceased, photographer father is a brand new unused camera. But not any camera: this is a motion camera.

He quickly wants to put it to use, but what can he film? There are no steam trains coming into stations in his village; no camels walking past pyramids; just a muddy street. The only things moving are a couple of nesting storks but on film they look as small as fleas. But then Motl makes another discovery. He removes the lenses from two cameras and films the storks swooping into their nest. Feeling inspired to further experimentation he attaches a lens to a thread and zooms in and out as he films villagers going about their business.

But it is one of the villagers, Anna, who takes things to another level. Calling Motl's film 'boring and stupid' she takes a pair of scissors and cuts it up into pieces. She then re-assembles the pieces into a different order. She has just edited the film so that it tells a story.

Unfortunately it is a story no one wants to see. People will not pay to see a film of an ugly butcher who has a reputation for putting mice in his pies. So Motl makes another film. With the backing of the local timber merchant he employs actors and musicians and makes his first feature film. He has plenty of ideas for stories and further technical advances but becomes frustrated at having to make 'Jewish movies'. His father once tried to explain to him what it is to be Jewish. "It isn't about nationality", he explained, "because there are Jews all over the world.

And it isn't about religion because you can choose what laws to obey. In order to be Jewish you just have to think that you are Jewish." Motl replied, "In that case, I don't think that I am Jewish".

In order to expand his horizons he goes to America, Hollywood, where Molt becomes Maurice. With flash forwards we know that he is a tremendous success, but there was always sadness at what he had to leave behind to fulfil his dreams.

Travelling Light is a warm and touching story of how a virtually penniless layabout from Eastern Europe became a major player during the golden age of Hollywood. It would be hugely challenging to produce but it is a beautifully told story that I am sure would have any audience entranced.

THE TREE OF KNOWLEDGE
Author: Jo Clifford
Publisher: Nick Hern Books
ISBN NO: 9781848422353
Cast: 2M 1F
Type: Full Length

This is a play that finds the 18th century philosopher David Hume and his friend, economist Adam Smith, in the early part of the 21st century. Jo Clifford admits that the hardest part for her in writing this commissioned play was that she knew absolutely nothing about David Hume. Then, when she did some research, she found that she couldn't understand him. Her inspiration came when she was reading one of his essays in which he stated with utter conviction that there is nothing at all after death. What if he was wrong? What if he was wrong about everything? And what would Adam Smith make of today's free market economy if he saw it in action?

This is the promising scenario that finds Hume and Smith pondering how their hearts can be beating if they are dead. They take snuff. They sneeze therefore they are.

They are joined by Eve who has recently died from a heart attack. She shows Hume the factory where she worked that made silicon chips for computer games in the 1970s. They are crude devices but they herald the start of a revolution. In a break from the rather wordy script there is some humour gained from Smith going clubbing and popping an ecstasy tablet. Once he regains the ability to speak he enthuses about the power of the internet. He is excited by its potential to enable him to 'peruse the greatest sages the world has ever known.' But mostly he is excited by the possibility of sex with young men.

There is quite a lot of sex in this play. It appals Hume but, initially, delights Smith until he tires of it and seeks tenderness instead. He is disillusioned with the world and America in particular, that 'hopeful experiment in equality and liberty and the rights of man', where you can now buy a machine gun off the shelf to kill them. The world has not lived up to the expectations of these men.

Jo Clifford once condemned a play in the Scottish press having neither read nor seen it. The title, Three Guys in Drag Selling Their Stuff, and the publicity was enough for her to decide that the play was about as politically correct as The Black and White Minstrels. I know the author of this play that so upset her; he recently celebrated the fortieth anniversary of his relationship with his same sex partner. I know that he has knowledge of his subject and that the play was warm, funny and not in any sense disrespectful of the characters. I mention this because I feel that my judgement of Jo Clifford's script may be adversely affected by this incident, but I suppose I can state that at least I took the time to read it. Personally, I found the humour rather base and the long passages of speech a bit self indulgent. I'm not sure that descendants of Hume or Smith will be pleased with how their ancestors have been portrayed, but I'm sure the play will have some appeal in fringe theatres including, perhaps, the theatre that staged the play that angered Jo Clifford so much.

TRIPTYCH

Author: Edwin Preece
Publisher: Drama Association of Wales
ISBN NO: 9781908575081
Cast: 2M 1F
Type: One Act

This play features subjects of three paintings: Girl Sipping Tea, Boy in Trunks and Boy Juggling Oranges. Talking directly to the audience they each describe how they were discovered by a famous artist, Benedict St Jude, and became famous themselves – but only by the names of the painting rather than their own names.

The girl became Benedict's lover but he seemed to grow tired of her and introduced her to Boy in Trunks with whom she began a relationship. Then Benedict mixed things up a bit by introducing them both to Boy Juggling Oranges. His reasons are obscure at first but we eventually learn that his plan was to bring his three most famous subjects together in a triptych – a painting in three interlinked parts – the link being a representation of the relationship that developed between the three.

This is an unusual one act play that would make an interesting piece for three young actors to perform.

TUESDAY AT TESCO'S

Author: Emmanuel Darley with English text by Matthew Hurt and Sarah Vermande
Publisher: Nick Hern Books
ISBN NO: 9781848422254
Cast: 1M
Type: One Act

Pauline spends every Tuesday with her father. After tidying up and doing his ironing she gets the shopping trolley out and takes her father to Tesco. This has been the routine ever since her mother died; going round every Tuesday to do the things her father can't or won't do for himself.

When she arrives her father calls out a greeting. "Hello Paul", he will say. "Pauline, now", she will reply. "Pauline, Okay."

They go to Tesco and people stare. Unlike at her local branch, she is known here. People remember her when she was Paul. Her father keeps his distance. He reads the labels on tins and pretends they are not together. She calls him and he comes close to her and tells her that he can see his stubble; that she looks nothing like a woman – too broad shouldered. Then he moves away.

There is a good deal of repetition in Pauline's speech whilst she describes the experience in the supermarket, emphasising the repetitive nature of the routine, but they break the habit later and stop for a drink on the way home. After this they bump into a friend of Pauline's father, a woman that Pauline doesn't know, and through her remarks we get the first hint that maybe Pauline's father is not quite as hostile as his behaviour towards her might suggest.

But then, just when we think there may be a reconciliation, there is a dramatic twist. Pauline works on the street and, when she is attacked, her names, both Paul and Pauline are printed in the newspaper. Here, the story ends abruptly.

Pauline's story is a complex tale, simply told, resulting in a moving piece of theatre.

UMLAUT, PRINCE OF DUSSELDORF
Author: Michael Green
Publisher: Samuel French
ISBN NO: 9780573122910
Cast: 5M 2F + extras
Type: One Act

The latest addition to Michael Green's Course Acting series finds a hapless theatre company attempting a condensed version of Hamlet.

If you have seen anything of this series then you will know what to expect. Actors bodge their lines, enter at the wrong time and take the wrong exit; sound technicians play the wrong cues, or the correct cues at the wrong time. Props become weapons as Umlaut attempts his 'to be or not to be' speech accompanied by jets of smoke that all but hide him from the audience and the sound of Deutschland Uber Alles played at the wrong speed.

I subscribe to the Les Dawson Piano Playing theory that to appear that bad you have to be very good indeed and, if it were done well, I am sure an audience would laugh at this play. One scene, where Umlaut was unable to remove his dagger from its sheath, and was, therefore, forced to deliver the line, "Is this a handle I see before me?" even made me smile, but I do wonder if the world already has enough plays about incompetent actors.

UP POMPEII
Author: Miles Tredinnick
Publisher: Josef Weinberger
ISBN NO: 9780856763380
Cast: 6M 5F
Type: Full Length

Miles Tredinnick has had quite a varied career. His first stage play, Because of Mr Darrow, was performed in London twenty years ago;

he was a writer on the BBC comedy Birds of a Feather; he has written a novel and, under the pseudonym of Riff Regan, is the leader singer in a pop group. However, it is his experience as co-writer of a Frankie Howerd TV special called Superfrank that best qualifies him to create a stage play from the TV programme that starred the aforesaid comedian.

The script suggests that, as the audience are taking their seats, Senna the Soothsayer should wander amongst them uttering "Woe, woe and thrice woe": this should get them in the mood for what is to come. In the first scene we meet Erotica, the master's teenage daughter, who is pre-occupied with writing on a stone tablet. She explains that this is all the rage: her servant will take the tablet to her friend who will compose a reply for the servant to bring back. It's called "slating", explains Erotica but, just in case anyone in the audience didn't get the joke, her mother suggests shortening the message and calling it "texting".

From what I can remember, when I saw this on TV I was always rather impatient for the preliminaries to be over and for Frankie Howerd to appear so that it might get going and, reading this script, my feeling was the same but we don't have to wait long for Head Slave, Lurcio, to appear and begin "the prologue".

Of course he never quite gets round to delivering the prologue as we dive straight into the saucy picture-postcard type gags and a plot that involves Lurcio's master, Ludicrus Sextus, arranging a clandestine meeting with the enticing and very much up-for-it Suspenda.

The script is 113 pages, which is far too long, but audiences who yearn for humour reminiscent of 1970s BBC prime time comedy will find it here in abundance. With all adaptations of TV comedies the audience expect to see the actors do imitations of the stars who made the roles famous and this is especially the case with Up Pompeii as it relied so much on Frankie Howerd for its success. The author helps, even including catchphrases such as "Please yourself", but I can't help feeling that the actor cast as Lurcio in this adaptation will face a very difficult task indeed.

VISITORS
Author: Scott Marshall
Publisher: Kenyon Deane
ISBN NO: 9780715504192
Cast: 3F
Type: One Act

I have already recommended a number of Scott Marshall's festival-ready one act plays in these pages. As a leading adjudicator in GODA he would be expected to know what works well, and in this play he has produced what I believe to be his best script to date.

Visitors is a comic masterpiece as the three characters, Patience, Grace and Charity, speak as virtually one voice discussing all manner of visitors. The pace is quick fire as the three of them start, finish, and provide the middle bits, of each other's sentences. Subjects include: Gary, whose amorous tendencies after a glass or two of brandy are not entirely unwelcome; the vicar and his somewhat randy dog (or should that be the somewhat randy vicar and his dog) and figures from history, the bible and Hollywood. All of them have one thing in common: they have paid someone a visit.

This is the sort of play that leaps off the page. It is easy to imagine this on stage but requires great skill on the part of the director and actors. Whilst very alike in many ways the three characters do have their differences and it is important that their individual personalities are not lost in the pace of the piece. It would be worth the effort though: done well this play is a sure fire winner.

VOYAGER
Author: Tony Rushforth
Publisher: Samuel French
ISBN NO: 9780573122941
Cast: 2M 3F
Type: One Act

We are on the deck of a cruise liner sailing the Baltic. I wish: I'm reading this aboard a decrepit old substitute train (the usual one has broken down), the seats are rock hard and we are crawling through a barren winter landscape with no heating. Still, to look on the bright side, at least the overcrowding is keeping us warm! Back to the Baltic, and we meet Margot and her mother, Isabel. Margot is the reluctant voyager of

149

the title, persuaded to accompany her mother because the ports on the itinerary are interesting enough for her to put up with sharing a cabin.

Then a gentleman of Isabel's age (seventy-ish) introduces himself. He invites them to have drinks with him after dinner which they accept, but Margot soon excuses herself leaving the pair to get to know each other. Isabel is a widow and Stephen is a widower. We sense romance in the air and Isabel soon stakes her claim but, unfortunately for her, it is Margot that interests Stephen.

A few days pass and Margot has to break the news to her mother. It doesn't go well. She describes the conversation to Stephen as "locking antlers", but she is her own woman and is happy to make a decision regardless of what opinion her mother might hold.

This play was first performed in 2011 which I find quite surprising and I wonder if it was written some time ago. Apart from a reference to Stephen keeping up with the times because he has a Walkman (a piece of technology already all but obsolete), the idea that Stephen should be shocked by the suggestion that he and Margot live together rather than marry seems quite old fashioned even for someone of his age. But being old fashioned gives it a certain charm and I'm sure that this is a one act play that many audiences will enjoy.

WALKIES
Author: Jane Lockyer Willis
Publisher: Spotlight Publications
ISBN NO: 9781907307409
Cast: 2M 1F
Type: One Act

Steve is a vagrant living in a cardboard box in the woods. Jen is a middle class, middle aged woman who takes a daily walk in those same woods. Steve stops her and makes a complaint about her dog. Jen insists that she doesn't have a dog. Steve insists that she does.

Walkies is bordering on Theatre of the Absurd but it doesn't quite seem to come off. As a result it is difficult to believe in the characters and impossible to believe that Jen would accompany Steve back to his cardboard box where they sit together drinking whiskey out of glass tumblers.

The concept is nice but I believe that either the story needs to be more rooted in reality or it needs to go further down the path of the surreal.

WASHINGTON SQUARE
Author: Adapted by Richard Hills from the novel by Henry James
Publisher: New Theatre Publications
ISBN NO: 1840945141
Cast: 3M 5F
Type: Full Length

Washington Square was first published in 1880 and remains one of Henry James' most popular stories.

Catherine Sloper is in her twenties and the right age to be marrying, according to her aunt, Mrs Penniman. As luck would have it there is a young man who seems rather taken with Catherine and Mrs Penniman thinks that Morris Townsend would make an ideal husband. Catherine is not so keen on the idea whilst her father, Mrs Penniman's brother, Dr Sloper, is dead set against it. He believes that Morris is sure to be after Catherine's money.

As if to confirm this Morris proposes, even though he has only known Catherine for five days, and, somewhat surprisingly, she accepts. The situation is rather intriguing: Catherine is reasonably wealthy as a result of money left to her by her mother, but she stands to become considerably richer when her father dies. If she marries Morris her father will change his will and Catherine will not get a penny. Catherine suggests that they delay the wedding hoping that her father might change his mind but Morris wants to marry immediately. He tells her that he is not interested in the money and this is enough to convince Catherine of his love for her. We will later learn that it was more to do with an immediate need for access to money, even if it meant losing the chance of a greater fortune at a later date.

Dr Sloper duly changes his will but also asks Catherine to accompany him on a trip to Europe. When they return she is even more determined to marry Morris but there has been a change: he no longer wants to marry Catherine unless it is with her father's consent. It seems that his eyes are now on the greater prize. Catherine refuses and they break off the engagement.

Ten years now pass during which time the pair have had no contact. Dr Sloper has died before he could change his will back in favour of

Catherine and the money has gone to charity, but Morris still has his eyes on Catherine's money, even if the amount is less than he had hoped.

The story reaches a triumphant climax when Catherine sends Morris packing. She then has some packing of her own to attend to as she prepares for another trip to Europe: but this time it will be just her and her money.

Richard Hills captures the spirit of Victorian melodrama brilliantly. This is a script that that could very well have been written a century and a half ago with the protagonists being terribly polite despite their obvious hatred for each other. The characters are well developed and the story moves along at just the right pace to allow the audience to read between the lines and form their own ideas about the characters' intentions. A very well written play.

WHAT LOVE IS
Author: Linda McLean
Publisher: Nick Hern Books
ISBN NO: 9781848423008
Cast: 1M 2F
Type: One Act

Two older people, Jean and Gene, are coming to terms with the fact that they are no longer able to look after themselves. Meanwhile, Jeanette is coming to terms with her responsibility to look after Jean and Gene. Is that what love is - responsibility?

"She has my smile." says Jean. "Almost." says Gene, "But it stops, just there. Before it lights her eye." Then, "You smiled at her. You smiled at her when you could have been smiling at me." What emotion! Whilst much of this sugar coated conversation is reminiscent of a pair of love-struck teenagers, if you read between the lines it is clear that Gene and Jean have suffered their fair share of pain over the years. But Gene remembers very little, is easily distracted and, when Jeanette arrives, almost reverts to childhood.

There is a lot of delicate walking-on-eggshells as Jeanette tries not to say the wrong thing but then there is the occasional deliberately hurtful comment that reveals her frustration at her situation. Every line is packed with emotion, much of it pulling vigorously at our heart strings but there are also moments of light relief. For example, when Jeanette leaves the room leaving her platform shoes behind there is a glorious moment when Gene steps into the shoes and gives us a verse of David Bowie's Jean Genie.

Perhaps the excitement of this silliness was too much though. We almost end with tragedy but instead life moves on even if death seems to come nearer.

This is such a beautiful written play. Anyone would need to have a heart of stone not to rejoice in the love that Jean and Gene still have for each other and be moved by the fact that, though their lives may be nearly over, they still celebrate the time they have left together.

WIT'S END (FEMALE VERSION)
Author: Neil Rhodes
Publisher: Drama Association of Wales
ISBN NO: 9781908575104
Cast: 2F
Type: One Act

Nicola Phillips is a famous TV broadcaster. A popular choice to present reality shows, she climbed her way to the top relying on her wit, intelligence and talent. Or did she?

As the play begins she is in her expensive flat poised to sign a new lucrative contract when she has a visitor. Enter Delia, the demon. No, really. Delia is a representative of the devil himself and has some bad news for Nicola. Sixteen years ago, when Nicola was a student, she was lying in the bath at the end of a grotty day and exclaimed that she would sell her soul to be famous. Delia is there to collect payment.

At first Nicola is understandably incredulous but, as it becomes clear that Delia really is who she says she is, we see a feistiness in Nicola that makes us wonder if she needed any help getting to the top. However, Wit's End is not a complicated play. It is just a simple comedy with a couple of decent parts which should get the audience smiling.

THE WITNESS
Author: Vivienne Franzmann
Publisher: Nick Hern Books
ISBN NO: 9871848422506
Cast: 2M 1F
Type: Full Length

"You are allowed to talk in the quiet coach. Middle aged women can shout about Martin Amis all the way to Kings Cross." This is the opinion of Alex and her excuse for why she is so tired and unappreciative of her father's jollity.

Years ago Joseph was taking photographs in Rwanda for a newspaper and it was one of Alex, crawling amongst the corpses of her murdered family, that won him an award. He adopted her, brought her back to his Hampstead home and became her father. Now she is back from her first year at university and worrying about the increase in her father's girth due to a massive increase in his consumption of cheese products. Despite Alex's tiredness it is an affectionate homecoming: it seems (like) they have missed each other.

This is the type of play that builds slowly. With each scene we learn a little more about Alex and Joseph whilst also becoming curious as to what is to come. Alex gets a summer job at Sainsbury's. Joseph is being pestered to put on an exhibition of his work. Then comes the first bombshell. Alex has dropped out of university and is living in a bedsit in Cambridge, getting by on the wages from working in a bar. Joseph demands an explanation and we begin a journey into their past.

I have written before about the importance of making an audience care about the characters, otherwise they will not care what happens to them. In The Witness, Vivienne Franzmann subtly places Joseph and Alex into our hearts within the first couple of scenes, the warmth of their affection for each other soon to be chilled by the revelations of the past.

Joseph and Alex were not the only ones alive that time in Rwanda. There was also Simon. He was edited out of the photograph and blocked out of Joseph's memory until five years ago when he got in touch to say that he believed he was Alex's brother. Why the delay before Joseph accepted his request to visit them? Why does he resent this boy so much? Joseph accuses Simon of being an impostor and of having sex with Alex. He offers him a huge sum of money to go away. Why is Joseph so frightened of Simon? The answer is in the title of the play. Simon saw what happened on that day of the photograph; how Joseph got his award winning photograph at the price of integrity. It is about to cost him a whole lot more.

The Witness is a remarkable play: one that gets under your skin and has you thinking about it for days afterwards; the dramatic equivalent of a page turner. Great stuff!

THE WOLVES OF WILLOUGHBY CHASE
Author: Adapted by Russ Tunney from the book by Joan Aiken
Publisher: Nick Hern Books
ISBN NO: 978184842338
Cast: Minimum 3M 2F
Type: Full Length

There are no wolves in Britain. But what if were? What if they entered Britain via a tunnel under the English Channel to escape the bitter cold of mainland Europe? This is the premise of Joan Aitken's 1962 novel set in in an alternative history of England where the fictional King James III reigned in the nineteenth century.

Bonnie lives in the remote Willoughby Chase where she is being cared for by her distant cousin, Miss Slighcarp, whilst her parents are away on a sea voyage. Another cousin, Sylvia, is on the way to stay with them but the train is halted by wolves in the snowy countryside. A kind gentleman, Mr Grimshaw, tells Sylvia not to worry; the wolves seldom eat passengers.

At Willoughby Chase Miss Slighcarp is revealing herself to be a most evil guardian but Bonnie is a spirited girl who knows how to stand up for herself. Mr Grimshaw has fought off the wolves but then managed to knock himself out whilst retrieving his suitcase. He is brought to Willoughby Chase with Sylvia where he regains consciousness having apparently forgotten his identity.

Miss Slighcarp soon begins to make her presence felt: she dismisses all the servants save one; she sends Bonnie's toys away; she instructs that the girls are to have the plainest of foods whilst she enjoys oysters and champagne, and she locks Bonnie in a cupboard for a minor misdemeanour.

There is worse; much worse. Miss Slighcarp and Mr Grimshaw are conspiring to alter the will so that they inherit the house and everything in it once Bonnie's parents are dead; and the guardian (she) has assurances that the ship they are sailing on is not seaworthy and bound to sink.

Bonnie and Sylvia are sent away to an orphanage where life is miserable until they are rescued by Simon, the servant that Miss Slighcarp did not dismiss. He helps the girls get to London where Bonnie sees her father's solicitor who sets us on our journey to a happy ending.

This adaptation makes for good family entertainment though I am uncomfortable with some parts of it. For example Mr Grimshaw is given to peppering his speech with dated racial stereotypes which I imagine would bemuse children and embarrass their parents. However, a running theme of an obsession with cheese and a few scripted asides is certainly bound to please.

WUTHERING HEIGHTS
Author: Lucy Gough – adapted from Emily Brontë
Publisher: Nick Hern Books
ISBN NO: 9781848422186
Cast: 3M 4F
Type: Full Length

Adaptations seem to be all the rage at the moment: the latest batch of plays that I received for review did not include any original works! This is actually the second adaptation of Wuthering Heights that I have received since I started reviewing scripts for Amateur Stage but what surprises me is how different it is from the first one.

Like April De Angelis, the author of the previous script that I reviewed, Lucy Gough has remained faithful to the story. But where De Angelis used a narrator to ensure that no aspects of the storyline were omitted, Gough has chosen to represent everything through the text. This has resulted in the play being made up of no less than 40 scenes, some of them very short indeed, which any director will find a challenge in terms of keeping the play flowing.

The author has assisted in this matter, though, with very clear stage directions that deal with the passing of time well and this should help with fluency. An aspect of this adaptation that I particularly enjoyed is Gough's description of the character's' behaviour as being similar to dogs. They fight like dogs, growl like dogs and, on occasion, play like puppies. As someone who once had a Golden Retriever called Heathcliff I found this quite appropriate!

My Heathcliff, however, was a gentle and kind creature and nothing like the bitter revenge filled beast created by Emily Brontë and represented accurately in Lucy Gough's new adaptation.

THE XMAS FACTOR
Author: Alison Chaplin
Publisher: Arts on the Move
ISBN NO: 9781906153410
Cast: 16 Characters plus non speaking roles
Type: One Act for Children

We begin with the auditions and Stars 1 to 4 argue about how much work they have put in to get through. Star 4 kicks them off with 100 per cent but by the time Star 1 chips in we are up to 1 million per cent. The others are scornful: who ever heard of 1 million per cent?

Meanwhile, in Bethlehem, the Innkeeper is rushed off his feet. And, on top of everything else, the Son of God has apparently just been born in his stable. There's a lovely golden glow around him: they had better not be lighting fires with all that hay around.

Back at the audition and the four old timers are joined by Little Star whom they immediately see as a threat. She seems to genuinely be on "a journey" and the judges are going to love that. They get rid of her by convincing her that she has no chance because she doesn't have a USP (Unique Selling Point).

On a hillside overlooking Bethlehem the shepherds are playing I spy but it is quite boring when everything begins with S. Suddenly there is something beginning with A: an angel with tidings of great joy. The set off down the hill. The angel then spots Little Star and asks her to help guide the Three Wise Men to the stable. It seems the four old timers are auditioning for nothing.

We end with a traditional nativity scene but the off beat humour that has been evident to date comes to a quirky climax as one of the shepherds, feeling left out, wants to bear gifts just like the wise men. Maybe his special rock with a face on it? Maybe not.

The Xmas Factor is a lot of fun and I am sure that children will have no difficulty in relating to both the contemporary references and the traditional story. An excellent choice for anyone wanting to put on a Christmas show with a twist.

YES, PRIME MINISTER
Author: Antony Jay and Jonathan Lynn
Publisher: Samuel French
ISBN NO: 9780573115059
Cast: 6M 1F
Type: Full Length

I am not a big fan of stage adaptations of TV hits. They often don't transfer to the stage very well and the poor actors are usually expected to do impressions of the original cast members whilst playing the characters. The worst adaptations are where the writer simply cobbles together a few existing scenes and calls it a new play and this was my fear as I picked up this script. As I recently bought a compendium of scripts from the TV series in a second hand book shop, I would easily spot any regurgitation.

Fortunately, this is a new work. Some of it is familiar, yes, but we are in no doubt that we are in the present day. Jim Hacker is the prime minister of a coalition government struggling to keep his head above water when the whole of Europe is in crisis following the 'sub-prime' mortgage affair.

The play is set at Chequers and begins with the voice of a TV news reader announcing that Hacker is denying that the European Union is "sailing on the Titanic". Meanwhile, Hacker's Private Secretary, Bernard Wolley, and the Cabinet Secretary, Sir Humphrey Appleby, are discussing democracy. Sir Humphrey is all in favour of it: so long as democracy is a process to secure the consent of the people to policies of those qualified to make them. Of course, the people qualified to make the policies would not include the Prime Minister!

In the TV series Sir Humphrey almost always got his way in the end but he did it so subtly that Hacker thought it was his own idea. Never did he seem to question why each episode ended with Sir Humphrey smiling and uttering a satisfied "Yes, Prime Minister". The inevitability of this never detracted from the pleasure of seeing Hacker digging himself into a hole so big we cannot imagine how he is going to get out and, in this stage version, the spade is provided by the Kumranistan Foreign

Minister and the hole is a proposed pipeline that will run all the way from his own oil rich country to the UK taking a torturous route that takes in the whole of the European Community. It is a fantastic project but there is a condition: Britain will have to adopt the euro.

Sir Humphrey and Bernard have done their utmost to conceal this minor detail but Hacker learns of it from his Special Policy Adviser. It seems that this clause was inserted by Sir Humphrey for his own rather complicated reasons but Hacker manages to outmanoeuvre him and all looks rosy until the we find that the Kumranistan Foreign Minister has a condition of his own. One that involves what they euphemistically refer to as a euro-job. This is something that would be performed by a "Eurologist" or, rather, three of them: the prettier the better.

I am convinced that audiences will love this play. The utter confusion deliberately introduced by Sir Humphrey, mainly by speaking in very long paragraphs of multi-syllable words, Bernard's irritating but hilarious insistence on precision and the bureaucratic one-upmanship will be just as funny whether it is familiar or new and, although there are a few in-jokes to satisfy fans of the series, the whole audience will be swept along by the vibrancy of it all.

Of course Hacker cannot agree to the demands of the Kumranistan Foreign Minister (though he comes close) and it is Sir Humphrey who, as usual, saves the day. There will be no oil pipeline but this can be turned into a positive if they announce the decision as a way of fighting the global warming crisis. All they need is to make up some figures that make global warming seem much worse than it actually is. That would do, wouldn't it? Yes, Prime Minister.

PLAYS BY DAVID MUNCASTER

Published by New Theatre Publications
www.plays4theatre.com

CALL GIRLS
One Act - Comedy. 1m 4f

Call Girls is set in a call centre providing IT assistance to an
unspecified company. Three of the women get on well together and
'have a laugh' but for the last six months their happy little group
has been spoiled by the presence of Laura, an arrogant and aloof
troublemaker whose predilection for short skirts and low cut tops
probably has more to do with her getting the job than any particular
work skills. Thankfully this is Laura's last week and the others decide
not to let her go without letting her know exactly what they think of
her. Surprisingly it is Mary, normally the quietist member of the group,
who really lets rip but this uncharacteristic outburst could be the
biggest mistake of her life.

COMMUNITY SPIRIT
Full length - Farce. 8m 3f

The village of Snickerton has a new community hall and all the local
groups get together to organise an opening day that will never be forgotten. Pity Mel, the poor official from the local council who has to try
to keep apart the warring factions. There is Mike, the bombastic chair-
man from the choral society, who clashes with Chris, his deadly rival,
as well as just about anyone else who dare to disagree with him. Add a
couple of luvies from the am dram, some representatives of Churches
Together who couldn't be further apart, the leader of the cubs and
beavers who sees things in the night, and a host of other characters
including a caretaker with a very unfortunate name. Community Spirit
is a large cast play with eleven speaking roles and any number of none
speaking roles that starts out as a comedy of manners but by the end is
pure farce. Great fun for any theatre group looking to involve as many
of their members as possible

FRESH SHOWERS FOR THE THIRSTING FLOWERS
One Act Play   2f

Alice is a retired English teacher who is living a comfortable if rather lonely existence. A chance encounter with her neighbour's daughter re-awakens her passion to teach when she discovers that most unusual of things. A pupil who wants to learn! With a respectful nod to 'Educating Rita' this is a story of how a generation gap is easily bridged through the discovery of a mutual interest. All scenes are set in Alice`s living room which has minimal set requirements. The title of this play is taken from the poem 'The Cloud' by Percy Bysshe Shelley. Other quotes in this play are considered 'fair usage' and do not contravene copyright law but a licence is required to use the music specified.

MAD GARY'S FRUIT AND NUT CASE
Full length - Comedy Thriller.   4m 4f

It is a big day for Tommy. His lovely daughter Peaches has just married Lionel Looselips, the son of the biggest fruit and veg wholesale magnate in the whole of the county. Now Tommy can be assured that his market stall will always have the freshest, best value produce known to man. The wedding reception is a grand affair, friends and relations are joined by rivals who, for one day, put their differences aside; or do they? As the ceremonial fruit salad is consumed the guests start dropping like fruit flies. Who is responsible for this murderous act? What did they hope to gain? Who will be next? It's a job for "Mad" Gary Grasslover of the local constabulary.

This intentionally corny and ribald comedy/murder mystery provides plenty of laughs and opportunity for the audience to join in the fun by, not only trying to guess the murderer, but also by selected members being given characters to play.

MISSION IMPOSSIBLE
One Act - Comedy. 2m 3f

A meeting room, a flip chart, an enthusiastic facilitator, and four employees who are determined to give her a hard time. This is the background to Mission Impossible, a hilarious look at the corporate nonsense that anyone who has ever attended a team bonding session will know only too well. Ice Breakers and silly games do little to bond this team as the beleaguered facilitator gets tough to ensure that she gets the outcome she desires. Mission Impossible won the Congleton One Act Play Festival 2009.

WAITING FOR A TRAIN
Full length. 4f

Set on the platform of a rural railway station waiting for a train that never comes, this is a play about life, love and hope. The stark reality of living with schizophrenia is contrasted by the warmth and playfulness that exists between the main characters. With a degree of flexibility in casting and a set that would work better if it is suggested rather than detailed this is play should be relatively simple to stage at the same time giving the actors the opportunity to immerse themselves into characters that have great complexity and depth.

Published by YouthPlays
www.youthplays.com

THE KENNEL CLUB
One act - Comedy. 2m 2f

The Kennel Club is a short play set in rescue kennels. The four characters are dogs. Sally, the sensible Golden Retriever, Molly her nervous partner, Sam, a scatterbrained terrier and Bruno, the huge monster with a heart of gold. These diverse characters are all going to have to work together if Sally's plan to find them all new homes is going to work. The Kennel Club is a touching and funny short play that has won festivals on both sides of the Atlantic and is popular with both children and adults.

THE PUBLISHERS

Samuel French Ltd
52 Fitzroy Street
London W1T 5JR
P: 02073879373
W: www.samuelfrench-london.co.uk

Josef Weinberger
12-14 Mortimer Street
London W1T 3JJ
P: 020 75802827
W: www.josef-weinberger.co.uk

Stagescripts
Lantern House
84 Littlehaven Lane
Horsham
West Sussex
RH12 4JB
P: 0845 686 0611
W: www.stagescripts.com

New Theatre Publications
2 Hereford Close
Woolston
Warrington
Cheshire
WA1 4HR
P: 01925 485605
W: www.plays4theatre.com

Spotlight Publications
259 The Moorings
Dalgety Bay
Fife KY11 9GX
P: 01383 825 737
W: www.spotlightpublications.com

Cressrelles Publishing
10 Station Road Industrial Estate
Colwall
Herefordshire
WR13 6RN
P: (01684) 540 154
W: www.cressrelles.co.uk

Nick Hern Books
The Glasshouse
49a Goldhawk Road
London
W12 8QP
P: 0208 749 4953
W: www.nickhernbooks.co.uk

Oberon Books
521 Caledonian Road
London N7 9RH
P: 02076073637
W: www.oberonbooks.com

Lazy Bee Scripts
2 Wood Road
Ashurst
Southampton
SO40 7BD
P: 023 8029 3120
W: www.lazybeescripts.co.uk

All plays in this volume can be purchased via
www.amateurstagemagazine.co.uk

The only
monthly magazine
passionate
about
amateur theatre

amateurstage
PASSIONATE ABOUT AMATEUR THEATRE
www.asmagazine.co.uk
OCTOBER 2013

NEWS | TRAINING | COMMENT | NATIONAL DIARY | INTERVIEWS

going up
MUSIC THEATRE SOUTH
LIFT

IN THIS ISSUE
> Loserville is released
> Making press releases work
> Put the fun into fundraising
> Playscript reviews

amateurstage
PASSIONATE ABOUT AMATEUR THEATRE
www.asmagazine.co.uk
NOVEMBER 2013
£2.95

NEWS | TRAINING | COMMENT | NATIONAL DIARY | INTERVIEWS

nice work...
Chelmsford AODS
Crazy For You

IN THIS ISSUE
> Ticket sales - it's in the detail
> Interview with Philip Rooke
> Win a production - Royalty FREE!
> Playscript reviews

ISSN 0002-8957

www.ingramcontent.com/pod-product-compliance
Lightning Source LLC
LaVergne TN
LVHW021453080426
835509LV00018B/2265